Shocking and Scandalous

STORIES FROM THE BIBLE

CHALLENGING STUDENTS
TO SEE LIFE FROM GOD'S POV

MARY GRACE BECKER & SUSAN MARTINS MILLER

Standard
PUBLISHING
Cincinnati, Ohio

Shocking and Scandalous Stories from the Bible

Published by Standard Publishing, Cincinnati, Ohio
www.standardpub.com

Copyright © 2010 Mary Grace Becker and Susan Martins Miller

All rights reserved. Permission is granted to reproduce the Director's Commentary, scripts, and handouts for ministry purposes only—not for resale. All other portions of this book may not be reproduced in any form, except for brief quotations in reviews, without the written permission of the publisher.

Also available: *Dark and Disturbing Stories from the Bible*, ISBN 978-0-7847-2400-2, copyright © 2010 by Mary Grace Becker and Susan Martins Miller

Printed in: USA
Acquisitions editor: Robert Irvin
Project editor: Kelli B. Trujillo
Cover and interior design: Thinkpen Design, Inc., www.thinkpendesign.com

Our thanks for their assistance in the production of the videos for these books goes to: B-Communicated Inc., Cincinnati Christian Schools, Dayton (Ohio) Church of Christ, Hamilton (Ohio) Church of God, LifeSpring Christian Church, Nancy's Hallmark Store (Sharonville, Ohio), TAB Productions, and Bob Wallace.

All Scripture quotations, unless otherwise indicated, are taken from the HOLY BIBLE, NEW INTERNATIONAL VERSION®. NIV®. Copyright © 1973, 1978, 1984 by Biblica, Inc.™ Used by permission of Zondervan. All rights reserved.

Scripture quotations marked (*The Message*) are taken from *THE MESSAGE*. Copyright © by Eugene H. Peterson 1993, 1994, 1995, 1996, 2000, 2001, 2002. Used by permission of NavPress Publishing Group.

The content in this book is not reviewed by, licensed by, or affiliated with the Motion Picture Association of America in any way. PG-13 is a registered trademark of the MPAA.

ISBN 978-0-7847-2399-9

15 14 13 12 11 10   1 2 3 4 5 6 7 8 9

Contents

Dedication **4**

Making the Most of *Shocking and Scandalous Stories from the Bible* **5**

1. Blood Brothers (GENESIS 4:1–16) **13**

2. She Loves Me, She Loves Me Not (GENESIS 29:15–28) **26**

3. Gangland (NUMBERS 16:1–3, 16–21, 28–32, 35) **38**

4. Earth Angel (JOSHUA 2:1–15) **51**

5. The Ghost Whisperer (1 SAMUEL 28:3–20) **63**

6. Risky Business (2 SAMUEL 11:2–5, 8–11, 14–17, 26, 27; 12:1–7) **76**

7. Mean Girl (1 KINGS 21:1–19) **90**

8. Her Majesty's Secret Service (ESTHER 3:5, 6, 8, 9; 7:1–10) **103**

9. Extreme Rampage (MATTHEW 2:1–16) **117**

10. Resident Evil (MATTHEW 4:1–11) **129**

11. Dirty Dancing (MARK 6:17–29) **142**

12. The Mob (ACTS 6:8–15; 7:54–60) **154**

13. Under the Influence (ACTS 8:9–24) **166**

I highly endorse *Shocking and Scandalous* and *Dark and Disturbing Stories from the Bible*. These are comprehensive studies, and anyone, not just middle schoolers, will gain a better grasp of how to present these stories found in the Bible. They're told separately, yet fit together like a scriptural mosaic. The concepts are fabulous. There is no stone unturned, as the books answer questions with candor and yet provide encouragement, hope, and understanding—all while dealing with real-life issues.

— Chris Brownlow, community program coordinator of Colorado Springs, Youth Activities

Mary Grace Becker and Susan Miller beam a spotlight on PG-rated stories in the Bible—stories that portray lust, lawlessness, and violence. Using clear communication and a creative, contemporary format, they grab and hold the interest of middle schoolers. This curriculum equips middle schoolers to resist negative peer pressure and to follow God's prescribed path during a complicated period of life.

— Dr. Jim Dyet, board member and mentor, Jerry Jenkins Christian Writers Guild; retired curriculum editor and pastor

At times it's hard to reach young teens with God's truth because they can portray lack of motivation, disinterest, or boredom with church or spiritual issues. Look no further for the curriculum that will overcome those factors. *Shocking and Scandalous* and *Dark and Disturbing Stories from the Bible* is a powerful, truth-defining, and spiritually challenging curriculum certain to grip the heart of the young teen. A refreshing and thought-provoking delivery of spiritual truths set within the day-to-day tough stuff that young teens face. . . . Awesome!

— Jodi Hoch, middle school teacher and curriculum developer

This is a gem in the middle school curriculum world! Carefully planned lessons allow students to think through their own decisions and actions, connecting spiritual growth to the Bible stories many churches avoid—even though the salacious and disturbing stories of the Bible often attract young teenagers to the honesty and authenticity of Scripture. There is much to be learned in the Bible passages that are difficult and ugly; the authors have gone to tremendous lengths to ensure these lessons hit the issues young teens deal with in creative, entertaining, and respectful ways.

— M. Karen Lichlyter-Klein, pastor, Colorado Springs

Some may find it hard to believe that Mary Grace and Susan are adults! Their uncanny ability to connect with youth brings the Bible alive to a generation that sees it as outdated. As you can see in the faces of the teens in the videos, the core messages fill them with an excitement to dig into God's Word and his plan. If you know teenagers, get these books and check out the curriculum.

— Ron Luce, president, Teen Mania Ministries

For all the youth leaders who asked us for something more. Here it is.

—M.G.B. & S.M.M.

Making the Most of *Shocking and Scandalous Stories from the Bible*

Brice and Jason take extreme pleasure in teasing the girls.

Allison craves the attention and often rewards both boys with a friendly slap.

Jordan giggles at everything.

Miranda thinks she's above it all.

Jake refuses to admit he's interested in anything.

Every class discussion carries an undercurrent of wanting to fit in and be noticed.

Welcome to middle school! Your students are bursting with independence and often insist on making their own decisions. They are miles away from being elementary-aged kids, but at the same time, too many of them lack the foundation to make wise choices. They want what they value *in the moment,* but don't necessarily consider how it will affect life long-term. What's ethical depends on the situation . . . and what they want out of it. They're fixated on youth culture, media, and technology.

Middle schoolers crave relationships but don't always know how to build positive, supportive friendships. Whether innocent or naïve or just seeking to be different, students in this age group want to fit in *somewhere.* Increasingly, they're swayed by peers and have no fixed reference point to guide their decisions.

> These lessons are designed to be used in a variety of formats, such as a middle school Sunday school class, a junior high youth group meeting, or even a mid-week small group meeting.

> Throughout each lesson, you'll see **bolded words**. These are our suggestions of what you can **say** as you're facilitating the lesson and leading discussion. Don't treat these suggestions as a script—be natural as you say them or use your own words to communicate the same idea. You'll also see *italicized* possible answers following some of the discussion questions. These aren't the "right" answers—they're just ideas you can use to help students start talking or to zero in together on the key ideas of the study.

This is a tough crowd to lead anywhere—but even a tough crowd needs to hear God's truth. So how do you connect with them and connect them to the truth?

STORIES THAT MAKE GREAT MOVIES

Shocking and Scandalous Stories from the Bible emphasizes the authority of God's Word and how middle schoolers can come together to help each other stand strong. It doesn't use the recycled Bible stories kids have heard a bazillion times in Sunday school. Instead, it focuses on stories that leave you asking, "Is that *really* in the Bible?" The stories most curriculums avoid because of their "PG-13" content.

The Motion Picture Association of America describes a PG-13 motion picture as going beyond the PG rating in theme, violence, nudity, sensuality, language, adult activities, or other elements, but not so far that it reaches the restricted R category. PG-13 movies include some material that may not be suitable for children—and middle schoolers are no longer living in a childlike world.

The stories in *Shocking and Scandalous Stories from the Bible*—and our companion volume, *Dark and Disturbing Stories from the Bible*—will grab the attention of middle schoolers as they're developing values and will get your students to take a close look at moral and ethical issues that were relevant in Bible times and still are today. These include things like step-family relationships, broken trust, dating, hate crimes, illicit sex, alcohol abuse, and more. These Bible stories are not about model choices and feel-good moments; instead, most of them are about the *bad* decisions people make. The discussion-based lessons showcase the "me-first" attitude that got many Bible characters into trouble.

Shocking and Scandalous Stories from the Bible will give your students the tools they need to make better choices—godly choices—when they face PG-13-level challenges in their own lives.

RULES OF ENGAGEMENT

Shocking and Scandalous Stories from the Bible is full of opportunities for your students to interact and build strong relationships. They'll connect through dramas, discussions, challenges, group journaling, fun games, and prayer. Through these experiences, they'll discover that they're not alone—they can depend on each other, support each other, and stand strong together against the pressures of peers and culture.

But in order to develop these types of relationships, your meetings need to be a safe environment where participants feel free to express themselves openly without fear of ridicule or rejection. We suggest you establish some "rules of engagement" for your group. A great way to do this is to get the students involved in creating the rules of engagement so that they develop their own expectations for the best ways to interact with each other. Your group's list will be as unique as your students and the realities impacting them.

Here's a sample of what some Rules of Engagement could look like:
Rule #1: God is #1, second to none.
Rule #2: Meetings will begin and end on time. Don't be late!
Rule #3: Cell phones off.
Rule #4: You're important. We want to know what you think and feel.
Rule #5: There are no bad ideas.
Rule #6: What's said and done here stays here.
Rule #7: No complaining—let's find a solution instead.

Another approach is to explore Bible verses and use them as the basis for creating your group's Rules of Engagement. For example, participants could look up verses like these to develop their rules:

Colossians 3:12: Therefore, as God's chosen people, holy and dearly loved, clothe yourselves with compassion, kindness, humility, gentleness and patience. *(Treat each other with respect. We are a team!)*

1 Thessalonians 5:11: Therefore encourage one another and build each other up, just as in fact you are doing. *(Be positive.)*

Proverbs 12:18: Reckless words pierce like a sword, but the tongue of the wise brings healing. *(Think before you blurt something out.)*

Proverbs 18:13: He who answers before listening—that is his folly and his shame. *(Listen without interrupting.)*

Proverbs 8:33: Listen to my instruction and be wise; do not ignore it. *(Take your cues from what the Bible says.)*

Psalm 119:15, 16: I meditate on your precepts and consider your ways. I delight in your decrees; I will not neglect your word. *(Put effort into understanding what the Bible says even if you don't understand it at first.)*

Philippians 2:3: Do nothing out of selfish ambition or vain conceit, but in humility consider others better than yourselves. *(Think about what is good for the others in the class, not just for yourself.)*

As you create your rules together, ask all of your students and leaders to sign or initial the list and display it in your meeting area. This helps create buy-in and will serve as a tangible reminder of the group's commitment to one another.

> The **dramas** in this book are simple enough that you can select actors and have them read through and act out the skits without advance preparation. But if you've got a group of kids who are really into **acting,** you can recruit them ahead of each lesson and give them opportunities to practice the skits in advance.

HOW THESE LESSONS WORK

Teaching a lesson from this book isn't complicated. At the start of each lesson, you'll find a **Director's Commentary**—a section just for you that outlines the key ideas of the lesson and how you'll lead your students in exploring them. First you'll find the Scripture portion the lesson is based on along with the elements of the story that (we think) qualify it for its "PG-13 rating," a **Key Bible Verse**, and the lesson's **POV** ("point of view"). The POV is the learning focus—the main idea you want your students to take away from their exploration of God's Word. Using student-friendly language, the POV points to God's perspective and the connection between the Bible passage and students' real lives. You'll also find a simple chart at the beginning of each lesson that outlines what you'll do in each part of the lesson, how long it should take, and what you'll need to pull it off. Finally, to give you extra insight into the biblical content you'll be exploring with your group, you'll find a **Why Is This PG-13 Story in the Bible?** section that provides you with an overview of the Bible story and the ways you can connect it to the lives of your students.

> Add an element of fun to the dramas by stocking a one-size-fits-all **prop box** that your students can use to come up with an instant fun prop, costume, or sound effect for each lesson's drama. A run to a secondhand store or garage sale can yield hats, wigs, scarves, sunglasses, old cell phones, noisemakers, and more.

Each lesson is organized into three main parts:

Take 1—Movie Preview

Take 1 begins each lesson with an activity that sets up the day's Bible story in a relational way, such as through dramas, role-plays, icebreaker games, and hands-on projects. Each activity will lead into a lively discussion of modern-day moral or ethical dilemmas that echo the Bible story.

Take 2—Feature Presentation

Take 2 moves your group directly into the Bible story, where students will have a chance to examine the tough choices the people made and the consequences that resulted. Here you'll use an **Outtakes** handout that will help your students get to know the characters (**Cast**), the story's main points (**Movie Trailer**), and

Making the Most of *Shocking and Scandalous Stories from the Bible*

God's perspective (**POV**) on this situation. Students can read the Scripture passage (from *The Message*) on each Outtakes page, or they can read it in their own Bibles. Each Take 2 section also includes **Team Talk**—opportunities for participants to look more deeply into the Bible story in a small group setting. (Keep reading for more info on running these small groups.)

Take 3—Critics' Corner

Take 3 will wrap up your lesson by reinforcing the POV through reflective discussion, a fun team-building activity, and prayer. The light-hearted team-builder activity at the close of each lesson is a fun, high-energy way to help your students solidify their relationships with each other so that they can support each other in living out the day's POV.

OUT-OF-THE-BOX WAYS TO CONNECT SCRIPTURE TO LIFE

Along with fun icebreakers, dramas, team-builders, and insightful discussion questions, *Shocking and Scandalous Stories from the Bible* uses unique methods like an interactive DVD, group journaling, small group discussion, and teen mentoring to move beyond the typical "listen-to-a-leader-talk" approach to middle school youth meetings or Sunday school classes.

Interactive DVD

Each lesson provides you with an opportunity to connect with your media-savvy students by using a **DVD** to kick-start discussion. In some sessions, the DVD will be an onscreen version of that lesson's skit, so it'll be up to you which avenue you'd prefer. In other sessions, the DVD for that week will use footage of real-life students, just like yours, who are answering questions, doing activities together, or in hot-seat scenarios. These clips will serve as a catalyst to get your group excited to talk or to prepare them for an activity they're about to do.

In every lesson, the DVD option is meant to enhance and enliven the experience your students are having, so use it as a tool to help keep things exciting. And it may be your choice to do both: have your students act out the drama or answer the questions, then play the DVD. Compare your students to those in our sample video—or better put, let them compare themselves. (Prediction: there's a good chance your students will do some boasting!)

Create a Group Journal

Use a group journal week after week to build community, to allow time for students to reflect, and to create an ongoing record of what students are learning. In each lesson you'll find specific suggestions for things your group can record in its journal, like a question to answer, an idea to brainstorm together, something to sketch, or a choice to evaluate. It's important that you encourage everyone to contribute—it's a *group* journal.

Your group can create a journal in a variety of ways. Here are a few ideas to get you started:

> **Group size:** Even if you have only, say, ten participants, it's still important to have students break up into Team Talk small groups. But if you've got just six students or less, it's probably a good idea to have them stay together and discuss both sets of Team Talk questions.

- Use an *oversized newsprint pad*. Decorate the cover with markers and keep the pages in the pad.
- Treat *windows or mirrors* in your meeting area *as dry-erase boards*. Be sure to keep a generous supply of colorful dry-erase markers on hand. (If you use this method, take photos of what the group has written at the end of each study so you have a record of their thoughts.)
- Post *self-stick notes* on the walls. Use a variety of colors and sizes and let students create a fresh, striking visual display each time. (Collect all the notes at the end of each lesson!)
- Set up *large or medium-size white boards/dry-erase boards*. Use one or several so everyone can participate artistically.
- Get creative with *construction paper*. Let your students use paper, scissors, and glue to create pages each week that you can save and bind in an imaginative way.
- Write on pieces of *poster board*. Use various colors and build a big stack each week.
- Compile students' reflections in a *three-ring binder*. Create several pages each week, slip them into sheet protectors, and add them in.
- Make a *scrapbook* together. Get fun papers and other unique scrapbooking supplies, then have participants write directly on the pages or glue in small pieces of colored paper. If you want, add stamps, trims, stickers, and so on.

Team Talk Small Groups

Relationships are the engine that makes these lessons go—that's why each lesson includes a **Team Talk** section in which students can talk openly and candidly in smaller-sized groups. To make these discussion groups the best they can be, aim to have about four to eight students and an adult or older teen leader in each group. When a group is the right size, it will give students (especially the more quiet and introverted ones) an opportunity to open up and dig through the challenges of these Bible stories with others.

Encourage groups to spread out around your meeting area and find their own space to talk. Assign some groups to discuss the first set of questions ("Team Talk 1"), the remaining groups the second set ("Team Talk 2").

In some lessons, you'll see instructions to divide your students into gender-based groups called **Guy Talk** and **Girl Talk**. This occurs when the theme of the story has a sensual element or a clear female perspective. Middle schoolers are ready to wrestle with tough questions, but sometimes they'll feel safer in a just-guys or just-girls group. And, in some cases, it's just best to avoid awkwardness or inappropriate things being said. If your group is too small to divide, handle questions with sensitivity.

> To help your teen mentors be successful in their new roles, be sure to meet with them regularly to pray and talk over lesson points and to get a general feel for how things are going in their Team Talk groups.

Make sure to prep your small group leaders for their role in the Team Talk discussions by having them read the **Why Is This PG-13 Story in the Bible?** section before each lesson to give them extra insight into issues that may come into play during discussions.

Teen Mentoring

If you can, we strongly recommend that you recruit some mature Christian high school students to help with these lessons. Successful teen mentorship makes a positive difference in the lives of young twelve-, thirteen-, and fourteen-year-olds! Middle schoolers look up to older teens who have successfully navigated the middle school years and are closer to their age than parents and teachers. Likewise, teens learn valuable life skills from leading Bible study discussion among middle schoolers. Mentorship, however, is not for all teens. Teen mentors understand they are role models and leaders-in-training. Mentorship is a responsibility. With that in mind, here are a few things to consider with your teen leaders.

The Power of Parents

Always keep in mind a golden rule for working with middle schoolers: involve their parents and guardians. Welcome parents to drop by and review the curriculum. Ask them to attend from time to time and help with activities. Keep them in the loop! Look for opportunities for hallway conversations, send e-mail or text message updates, and make plenty of phone calls. Build a partnership that surrounds students with God's point of view.

- Be sure to choose godly high schoolers who want to make a difference and who can put the interests of others above their own.
- A successful teen mentor should be someone who's friendly, enthusiastic, insightful, honest, and self-confident. He or she should inspire younger teenagers to be themselves and to rise above negative stereotypes.
- Teen mentors should be responsible and show up each week on time and prepared to lead their Team Talk discussion group.
- Last, mentors should feel free to share personal adolescence stories. Teens who remember what it was like to be a middle schooler will build trust with your students. (However, discussions on dating, high school pranks, or slips in judgment involving sex, smoking, or alcohol and drug use are not appropriate for this age level and should be kept out of the discussion.)

READY TO GO!

You have the tools to help your students know God on a deeper level. You have the passion to see it happen. You fully expect that God is going to do something great with your middle schoolers.

So does he. ✘

1

Blood Brothers

Director's Commentary

NOW SHOWING: *Blood Brothers*

FROM THE BIBLE: Cain kills his brother Abel (Genesis 4:1-16).

RATED PG-13 FOR: jealousy and murder

POV: Your actions reflect your heart, so take responsibility for them from the start.

KEY VERSE: "As water reflects a face, so a man's heart reflects the man" (Proverbs 27:19).

The Lesson	Time	What you'll do . . .	How you'll do it . . .	What you'll need . . .
Take 1: Preview	15 to 20 minutes	Start off your lesson by introducing the theme with a relational, creative activity.	Option 1: Students act out "Web Attack" drama and discuss it.	Photocopies of "With Friends Like These . . ." script (pp. 23, 24); markers, group journal supplies (*Optional*: items from your prop box, lunch bags, and food; movie snacks for your audience)
			Option 2: Kids watch a DVD version of "Web Attack." Or, choose to do both.	*Shocking and Scandalous Stories from the Bible DVD*, TV and DVD player; markers, group journal supplies
Take 2: Feature Presentation	15 to 20 minutes	Dive into the Bible story and explore it together.	Small group and large group discussion	Photocopies of **Outtakes** (p. 25); poster board cut into half-circles, markers *Optional*: Bibles
Take 3: Critics' Corner	15 to 20 minutes	Help your students grasp God's point of view and wrap things up with a fun team-building activity.	Discussion, game, and prayer	Photocopies of **Outtakes** (p. 25); group journal; play money, drinking straws, offering basket or plate

WHY IS THIS PG-13 STORY IN THE BIBLE?

The Bible starts out so fabulously! God creates a bedazzling world and totally wants a relationship with humans. Then our stomachs sink when Adam and Eve listen to the lies of the serpent instead of God's truth (Genesis 3). And now, in chapter 4, we plunge into the first violent story of the Bible.

Cain and Abel each bring an offering to God. God approves of Abel's and ignores Cain's. Why? The description of Abel's offering (4:4) emphasizes that he brings God the best—the firstborn of his flock and the best part of the animals. Abel thoughtfully plans a sacrifice that shows how he feels about God. Cain, on the other hand, casually brings "some of the fruits of the soil" (v. 3). He's not careful to get it right or bring the best.

Fruits and vegetables are not the issue. Cain's haphazard, grudging offering shows his heart—which is not making an effort to please God. Nevertheless, God goes looking for Cain and interrupts his sulking. God assures Cain that if he simply does what is right, his offering will be accepted (4:6, 7). God bends over backward to let Cain know he has options other than sinning and sulking. But instead of accepting this second chance, Cain reveals what's deep in his heart: a jealous grudge against Abel. Cain seems to go straight out from his talk with God to lure his brother to a field, where he murders him.

Once again, God goes looking for Cain, and once again Cain tries to brush off God. Instead of taking responsibility, he has the gall to lie to God and this is the last straw. God curses Cain and banishes him. Has Cain figured out he has anything to be sorry about? Nope. He whines that the punishment is too harsh for the offense—murder—and worries he'll be killed in exile. True to character, Cain only thinks about what's in it for him, not what pleases God. But once again God is gracious and promises to protect Cain's life.

This Bible story will help your students see that choices have consequences, and their willingness to take responsibility for their choices affects their relationship with God.

Connecting with Community

Log on to www.shockingandscandalous.com to connect with other ministries:
- Check out a sample video of other students in action.
- Share with other leaders at the PG-13 forum about what's working in your ministry, what's not, or how you used *Shocking and Scandalous* this week.
- Or ask for input about other aspects of middle school ministry.

1: Blood Brothers

Take It to Your Students

Here are some key points to emphasize with your students during this lesson:
- Think about your motives when you don't get your way.
- Before you make a choice, consider what it says about you.
- Be ready to take responsibility for the choices you make, right or wrong. ✘

Blood Brothers: The Lesson

Take 1: Preview (15 to 20 minutes)

Setup: This activity will set up the day's Bible story in a relational way as your group witnesses some lunchroom friends turn on an honor student.

Set design: Create a relaxed atmosphere for *Preview*. Ask students to sit in a circle on pillows, seat cushions, or just on the floor. If you're choosing to do the drama live, your actors can perform it in the middle of the seating area. Popcorn or movie snacks will help set a movie mood.

Makeup and effects: For today's drama (and for others in this book) consider stocking a one-size-fits-all prop box your students can rummage through to come up with an instant fun prop, costume, or sound effect for the day's drama. A run to a secondhand store or garage sale can yield hats, wigs, scarves, sunglasses, old cell phones, noisemakers, and more.

Props: Supplies for the journal option you've chosen, markers; 3 copies of the "With Friends Like These . . ." skit (pp. 23, 24); or the *Shocking and Scandalous Stories from the Bible DVD* and a TV with DVD player; or both. (*Optional*: items from your prop box, lunch bags, and food; movie snacks)

QUIET ON THE SET

To launch the lesson:
- Welcome everyone to the group. Use first names or preferred nicknames and introduce visitors. (Be sure to have everyone's names memorized by your next meeting.) After your students have had some time to socialize, pull them in and have them get comfortable.
- Go over your Rules of Engagement. These class-determined rules help young teens honor each other and give them the freedom to be truthful without

ridicule. (See the Rules of Engagement suggestions on p. 6 for more information.)
- Review the journaling component you've chosen for your group. (See the Create a Group Journal explanation on p. 10 for more information.)

ACTION

Either have students perform the "With Friends Like These . . ." skit, watch "With Friends Like These . . ." on the *Shocking and Scandalous Stories from the Bible* DVD, or do both. If you choose to have students perform the skit live, give copies of "With Friends Like These . . ." (pp. 23, 24) to your student actors and have them prep by reading through their parts a time or two. Also, invite the actors to rummage through the prop box for items to enhance their performance.

> If you want, make a video of your students' live performance of "With Friends Like These . . .". Play it back later, perhaps for the entire church!

PLAY BACK

Spend time reflecting on "With Friends Like These . . ." with your group by using the discussion suggestions below. As students talk, don't edit their responses—allow them to discuss freely. Have a volunteer write "With Friends Like These . . ." and today's date on your group journal and then record the group's impressions and suggested endings. Aim to give every student the opportunity to comment or to journal, even if it's just to write their initials to show their agreement with what others have written.

> You may want to break into small groups (such as just guys or just girls groups) for the journaling, discussion, or both.

Now for a little soul searching. You get to decide what Makayla will do.

Use these key questions to get the discussion going:

- **Makayla has a decision to make. What thoughts might be running through her head as she wrestles with her choices?**
- Is invading Stacy's locker a) just having fun; b) not good, but not bad either; or c) a form of bullying? What would Stacy say?
- What do you think Makayla will ultimately do? Why?
- What would *you* do in a situation like this?

1: Blood Brothers

Continue the group's exploration by saying something like: **Great discussion. We see how jealousy escalates tension into anger, which may result in others getting seriously hurt.**

In today's Bible story, two brothers face crippling tension. When one of them blows it, both pay the price. Up next, today's award-winning biblical feature, *Blood Brothers*. ✘

> The **bold** indicates things you can say to your group as you teach. Feel free to use our suggestions or communicate similar ideas in your own words.

TAKE 2: Feature Presentation (15 to 20 minutes)

Setup: Students will take a close look at the story of Cain and Abel and discuss taking responsibility for actions.

Props: Photocopies of **Outtakes** (p. 25); markers, and pieces of poster board cut into large half-circles

(To prepare the half-circles, cut a single large circle from each piece of poster board, then cut each circle in half.) *Optional:* Bibles

QUIET ON THE SET

Pass out copies of **Outtakes** (p. 25), one per student. *Optional:* Have students grab their own Bibles.

ACTION

Use **Outtakes** to introduce and teach the Bible story. First, briefly introduce the **Cast** and make sure your students know who's who. Next, use the **Movie Trailer** to cover the highlights of the Bible background and story. Then read the Bible story (Genesis 4:1-16) out loud from **Outtakes** or have a volunteer read it. If you prefer, ask students to read the passage aloud from their own Bibles.

PLAY BACK

Divide your group into small teams for discussion with an adult or older teen leader for each group; see the Team Talk Small Groups section on pp. 10, 11 for insights on how best to form the right-sized teams. Assign about half of the teams to explore Cain and Abel's actions (Team Talk 1 below) and the other half of the teams to explore God's actions (Team Talk 2). Remind group leaders to be ready to enhance discussion with insights from **Why Is This PG-13 Story in the Bible?** (p. 14). Also, give each team markers and a half-circle on which they can record the actions and emotions they think are in each character's heart.

Let's dig deeper into the *Blood Brothers* plot. We'll examine the motivations behind the actions we just read about.

Team Talk 1: Get into the heads of Cain and Abel.

- **What emotions do you see in Cain's heart? In Abel's? Write your ideas or draw some emoticons (smiley faces and similar stuff) to symbolize them.**
- **What actions do these emotions lead to? Write or draw these actions.** *(Abel brought a sincere offering. Cain lied and murdered.)*
- **What choices did Cain have?** *(To bring a sincere offering; to listen to God; to do the right thing.)*
- **How did Cain respond to God's efforts to communicate?** *(He was still only concerned about himself; he left God and murdered Abel.)*

Team Talk 2: Get into the head of God.

- **What emotions does God express in this story? Write your ideas or draw some emoticons (smiley faces and similar stuff) to symbolize them.** *(Pleasure and displeasure; determination)*
- **What actions does God take in response to those emotions? Write or draw these actions.** *(Actively seeks Cain; communicates; offers second chance)*
- **Why do you think God made such an effort to connect with Cain, even after he murdered his brother?**
- **Even when we fail God, as Cain did so spectacularly in Genesis, God still loves us. How does that make you feel?**

Bring the discussion teams back together. Briefly review the results of the various small-group discussions by looking at what students have written on their half-circles. Then hold two half-circles together, overlapping at the bottom, and point out that the shape of a heart emerges.

Continue your discussion as a large group by asking questions like:

- **In your opinion, where did Cain go wrong in this story?** *(Jealousy, murder, self-absorbed)*
- **How did God respond to Cain?** *(He kept trying to communicate.)*
- **What options do you have when anger and jealousy threaten to get the best of you?**

1: Blood Brothers

- **Why do you think this story about jealousy and murder is in the Bible?** *(This is a good opportunity to remind students of the Key Verse: "As water reflects a face, so a man's heart reflects the man" [Proverbs 27:19].)*

We wrote on half-circles and ended up with hearts. What's in our hearts shows in our actions. God knew Cain's heart, and what was in his heart mirrored his actions. Cain had options. He didn't have to let anger and jealousy rule his heart. He had choices. Let's look again at the choices made in this story.

Use these key questions to prompt more large-group discussion:
- **In your opinion, what were the top three bad choices in this story?** *(Wrong offering attitude; didn't take God's second chance; murdered and lied; thought only about himself; didn't take responsibility)*
- **What resulted from those choices?**
- **How do you think the story might have ended if Cain had taken responsibility for his actions from the start?**

Cain never learned his lesson. But you don't have to make the same mistake. What God is after is obvious: pay attention to what's in your heart and take responsibility. Your heart-actions speak loudly about the real you. ✘

TAKE 3: Critics' Corner (15 to 20 minutes)

Setup: Reinforce the points you want your students to take away from today's lesson.
Props: Group journal with entries from Take 1; **Outtakes** (p. 25); 12 play-money bills per team, drinking straws, offering basket

QUIET ON THE SET
Have students gather around the group journal and together review the endings they came up with for the "With Friends Like These . . ." skit.

ACTION
Consider the POV
Discuss the idea that jealousy and anger can cause real harm to family relationships and friendships; if you can, share an appropriate example from your own experience.

Then ask the group:

- **How do you think God wants us to treat each other?** *(Be patient, respectful, not insulting. Give praise and encouragement. Go gentle with criticism.)*

Draw students' attention to the **POV** on the **Outtakes** handout: *Your actions reflect your heart, so take responsibility for them from the start.*

Invite a volunteer to read aloud the alternative endings for the "With Friends Like These . . ." skit from the group journal. After each entry is read, ask your students to stand if they think the ending reflects today's POV. (If none of the endings from the journal fits, help the group write a new one.) Reinforce the POV one more time.

Understand God's Truth

Whether great or not-so-great, we are defined by the choices we make. Unless we take responsibility for them, we're stuck with the tempting pull of jealousy and other stormy emotions.

Ask the group:

- **What have we learned from today's story?** *(Like a virus, jealousy infects everyone. Cain was jealous of his brother. God offered him the chance to do what was right.)*

Consider having students talk in pairs about this next question in order to help them feel comfortable sharing a more personal response, then invite volunteers to share their thoughts with the larger group.

Ask:

- **Relationships with brothers or sisters are not popularity contests. What can *you* do to make things easier at home?**

Cain took on his brother in a jealousy-fueled death match . . . and Abel lost. Certainly, our actions are not as brutal as those in today's story. Nonetheless, our actions have a voice. Be on the lookout for ways you can own up and take responsibility for your own actions toward your family members and friends.

Teamwork

God's words from today's story say it all: "The voice of your brother's blood is calling to me from the ground" (Genesis 4:10, *The Message*). Are we our

1: Blood Brothers

brother's keeper? Absolutely! Let's be there to help each other put God's Word into action this week.

PLAY BACK

Wrap up the meeting with a fun team-building activity that will help students reflect on the idea of acceptable offerings. Then close in prayer.

Thoughtful Giving

Needed: play-money, drinking straws, an offering basket or plate
Goal: Use straws to pass money from player to player.

How to Play:

Say: **God makes clear that an acceptable offering reflects your heart.**

Form two or more game circles and ask players to kneel. (If your group is small, play with one circle.) Distribute one straw to each player. Place twelve play-money bills on the floor in front of the first player in the circle. Set the offering basket by the end player. On the count of "ready, set, go!" have groups pass money, one bill at a time, from one player to another, using straws only. (See if your students catch on to how this works! If not, demonstrate.) Player 1 will suck on her straw to "pick up" a bill and then release it, dropping it in front of the player next to her. Player 2 repeats the action. Play continues until the final player fills the offering basket with money. If bills drop along the way, play starts over. The circle that finishes first wins.

This offering game reminds us of Cain and Abel's offerings. One offering reflected a heart that was generous and wanted to honor God; the other revealed a heart that was stubborn and quickly became jealous. What do your actions reveal about your heart? How can your choices be like Abel's offering, showing the world a generous and loving person inside?

> To create cooperative teams for this activity and others in this book, use the following method (or one like it) to divide your group: write players' names on individual craft/Popsicle sticks and place them in a cup. When teaming up, grab a handful of sticks and randomly pull the desired number of sticks for each team.

> Save your play money to use in activities in lesson 13.

Option: Extend playing time, if needed, by adding pennies and dimes (fun, and a bit more straw-challenging!).

Close with Prayer

Ask your group to look again at **Outtakes** and repeat today's **Key Verse:** "As water reflects a face, so a man's heart reflects the man" (Proverbs 27:19). Then point out the *Verse-atility* paraphrase, a personalized version of the Key Verse: *Just as water reflects my face, so my heart shows the world the real me.* If time permits, jot the verse in the group journal and have everyone initial it. Encourage your students to keep God's truth front and center in their lives this week.

Invite students to share prayer requests, specifically those that connect with the main ideas of the lesson. Emphasize how jealousy keeps us stuck at square one and in no position to do what Scripture demands: to care for family and friends. Then say: **Remember, God gave a second chance to Cain. If you feel challenged that your choices haven't reflected the kind of person you really want to be, seek God's grace and forgiveness. He's always ready to give you a second chance.**

Verse-atility: *Just as water reflects my face, so my heart shows the world the real me.*

Pray for students' requests and, more generally, ask God to help your group live out the main ideas of today's lesson. ✘

With Friends Like These . . .

Characters: NARRATOR, MAKAYLA and ASHLEY: two middle school girls, DAVID: a middle school guy
Scene: Middle school study hall. The friends are also snacking as they get, at least, a little studying done.
Prop Suggestions: Select any props or costumes you want from the prop box. Also, if you want, use backpacks, sack lunches, and food (or just pretend!).
Director's note: The Narrator role is not used on the *Shocking and Scandalous DVD* videos. On-screen graphics are used at times instead. The narrator role allows you an additional role for the drama skits in this book.

SCRIPT

(DAVID enters school study hall and sees his friends ASHLEY and MAKAYLA sitting together at their usual table.)

NARRATOR *(this role is always "off-screen")*:
The first thing David sees when he enters the study hall are his friends bunched together at their usual table. Makayla waves him over.

MAKAYLA:
(waving) **Hey David, over here!**

NARRATOR:
David plops down, throws his backpack underneath the table, and digs into his backpack for something to snack on.

DAVID:
What's up?

ASHLEY:
(Taking a sip of her drink) **The Honor Roll was posted before lunch. It's on the wall outside Mrs. Pierce's office. Wanna hear who's on it?**

DAVID:
(shrugging—really doesn't care) **Nope. Don't wanna know. Besides, the same kids make that list every year.**

MAKAYLA:
You're just jealous, David.

DAVID:
(turning away) **I've got better things to do than sweat over grades, Makayla.**

MAKAYLA:
(rolling her eyes, irritated at her friend) **Really, like what?**

DAVID:
Whatever. *(Now rolls his eyes.)*

MAKAYLA:
You know, David, Mrs. Pierce tutors kids after school who want to do better. Stacy tried it and now she's number one on the honor roll. You should give it a try.

DAVID:
(fed up and annoyed) **E-*nough* with the brainiac talk, Makayla. Get over it.**

MAKAYLA:
Whatever. *(Now Makayla is getting annoyed.)*

(The table is silent for a few seconds as the students snack or look at their books, not sure what to say next. Then David continues…)

Hey, I've got an idea! Let's get into Stacy's locker. We can cover it with notes—"kiss up," "teacher's pet," "nerd"—stuff like that.

MAKAYLA:
See, you *are* jealous David! Besides, I thought locker combinations were supposed to be secret.

DAVID:
Dude, there's a way—trust me.

MAKAYLA:
(Feels uncomfortable with her friend's plan; hesitantly) I don't know. It sounds pretty mean.

ASHLEY:
Relax, Makayla. It's not like we're hurting anyone. Not really. *(To David)* What else you got?

DAVID:
(face brightening) We can put stuff up online—like pictures of her messed-up locker and stuff about how she thinks she's better than everyone else. *(Ashley laughs.)* That'd be hilarious!

NARRATOR:
Makayla doesn't feel comfortable with David and Ashley's plan—but she doesn't want them to start making fun of her too.

(Makayla is looking increasingly uncomfortable as David and Ashley talk. She is torn between looking "cool" to David and Ashley and following her conscience.)

ASHLEY:
(in a snobby, sarcastic voice) How 'bout this: "Stacy, a shining star, admired by know-it-alls everywhere."

MAKAYLA:
(grabbing her things and getting up to leave) This is gettin' nasty. I'm leavin'.

(Makayla picks up her bag from under the table and quickly heads off.)

DAVID:
(Turning to her, his words following her as she walks out of the room . . .)
What-ever, Makayla. Don't act like you're so innocent. Besides, you're the one who brought it up!

NARRATOR:
Makayla is amazed at how quickly things have turned. She's not a mean person and she doesn't see the point of picking on Stacy. Bullying is no fun—no matter what David and Ashley think. But is messing with Stacy that big of a deal? Really?

Ultimately, Makayla will need to make a choice.

(Skit ends; actors rejoin group.)

Permission is granted by Standard Publishing to reproduce this "With Friends Like These . . ." script for ministry purposes only (not for resale).

Outtakes

CAST

Cain: the older son of Adam and Eve; gave God vegetables for his offering
Abel: the second son of Adam and Eve; gave God animal meat for his offering
God

MOVIE TRAILER

- Adam and Eve have two sons, Cain and Abel, who grow up.
- Cain offers some vegetables to God. Abel brings an offering from the best of his animals.
- God rejects Cain's offering because it is not from his heart.
- God gives Cain a chance to change his heart and get things right.
- Cain chooses to murder his brother instead of straightening things out with God.
- God sends Cain into No-Man's Land.

Verse-atility: Just as water reflects my face, so my heart shows the world the real me.

POV: Your actions reflect your heart, so take responsibility for them from the start.
Key Verse: As water reflects a face, so a man's heart reflects the man (Proverbs 27:19).

BLOOD BROTHERS

Genesis 4:1-16 *(The Message)*
(We've added a few of our own comments **in bold** below.)

Adam slept with Eve his wife. She conceived and had Cain. She said, "I've gotten a man, with God's help!"
 Then she had another baby, Abel. Abel was a herdsman and Cain a farmer. Time passed. Cain brought an offering to God from the produce of his farm. Abel also brought an offering, but from the firstborn animals of his herd, choice cuts of meat. God liked Abel and his offering, but Cain and his offering didn't get his approval. Cain lost his temper and went into a sulk. **[Not exactly mature!]**
 God spoke to Cain: "Why this tantrum? Why the sulking? If you do well, won't you be accepted? And if you don't do well, sin is lying in wait for you, ready to pounce; it's out to get you, you've got to master it."
 Cain had words with his brother. They were out in the field; Cain came at Abel his brother and killed him. **[Cain, the murderer.]**
 God said to Cain, "Where is Abel your brother?"
 He said, "How should I know? Am I his babysitter?" **[Seriously—lying to God?]**
 God said, "What have you done! The voice of your brother's blood is calling to me from the ground. From now on you'll get nothing but curses from this ground; you'll be driven from this ground that has opened its arms to receive the blood of your murdered brother. You'll farm this ground, but it will no longer give you its best. You'll be a homeless wanderer on Earth."
 Cain said to God, "My punishment is too much. I can't take it! You've thrown me off the land and I can never again face you. I'm a homeless wanderer on Earth and whoever finds me will kill me."
 God told him, "No. Anyone who kills Cain will pay for it seven times over." God put a mark on Cain to protect him so that no one who met him would kill him. **[A second chance . . . awesome.]**
 Cain left the presence of God and lived in No-Man's-Land, east of Eden.

Permission is granted by Standard Publishing to reproduce this **Outtakes** handout for ministry purposes only (not for resale).

2 She Loves Me, She Loves Me Not

Director's Commentary

NOW SHOWING: *She Loves Me, She Loves Me Not*

FROM THE BIBLE: Jacob is tricked into marrying the wrong wife (Genesis 29:15-28).

RATED PG-13 FOR: deception and betrayal

POV: When things don't work out the way you expect, trust God's plan anyway.

KEY VERSE: "And we know that in all things God works for the good of those who love him, who have been called according to his purpose" (Romans 8:28).

The Lesson	Time	What you'll do . . .	How you'll do it . . .	What you'll need . . .
Take 1: Preview	15 to 20 minutes	Start off your lesson by introducing the theme with a relational, creative activity.	Option 1: Students get to know each other better by discussing the details of their own perfect day.	Photocopies of "Perfect Day!" (p. 36); pens or pencils, markers, group journal supplies (*Optional:* smiley face stickers)
			Option 2: Students watch the DVD version of "Perfect Day!" and discuss it. Or, choose to do both.	*Shocking and Scandalous Stories from the Bible* DVD, TV and DVD player
Take 2: Feature Presentation	15 to 20 minutes	Dive into the Bible story and explore it together.	Small group and large group discussion	Photocopies of **Outtakes** (p. 37); 4 or more large balloons, permanent markers *Optional:* Bibles
Take 3: Critics' Corner	15 to 20 minutes	Help your students grasp God's point of view and wrap things up with a fun team-building activity.	Discussion, game, and prayer	Photocopies of **Outtakes** (p. 37); group journal; large balloons, classroom furniture (*Optional:* additional balloons, pennies)

WHY IS THIS PG-13 STORY IN THE BIBLE?

Jacob is in a pickle, and even he can't deny the irony. Jacob, the younger twin, has taken advantage of his older brother Esau and gotten him to hand over the inheritance Esau was entitled to (Genesis 25:31-34). Then he tricks his old and blind father Isaac into giving him the blessing of the firstborn—the blessing intended for Esau (27:1-36). Birthright and blessing—Jacob schemes to snatch them both for himself and savors the prospect of enjoying the cultural privileges granted to an eldest son. But Esau's on a murderous rampage, so Jacob heads for the hills. His mother (and co-conspirator) Rebekah sends him to her brother Laban.

Laban offers Jacob a paying job. Smitten by Laban's younger daughter Rachel, Jacob promises to work seven years in exchange for marrying Rachel when the time's up. This is a generous price to pay for a bride, but Jacob doesn't cut any corners. So Jacob and Rachel make eyes at each other for seven years, and then Laban throws the customary huge party. It's only after the wedding and honeymoon night that Jacob discovers his father-in-law has sneakily slipped in his older daughter, Leah, in place of Rachel. Laban claims custom demands that the older daughter marry before the younger. We might wonder why he didn't mention this detail to Jacob seven years earlier or why he wasn't busy finding a husband for Leah. Was Laban planning this switcheroo all along?

The culture permitted multiple wives, so Laban proposes that Jacob also marry Rachel—and then work another seven years. Laban has Jacob over a barrel. Jacob still wants Rachel and now he has little to bargain with. A week after the tricky wedding to Leah, Jacob also marries the woman he loves. Although he was duped, Jacob keeps his end of the bargain and remains Leah's husband; together they have four sons. And even though he has Rachel now, Jacob keeps his word and spends another seven years working for Laban.

Later, Jacob goes on to become a patriarch of God's people. His twelve sons become the

> **Connecting with Community**
> Log on to www.shockingand scandalous.com to connect with other ministries:
> - Check out a sample video of other students in action.
> - Share with other leaders at the PG-13 forum about what's working in your ministry, what's not, or how you used *Shocking and Scandalous* this week.
> - Or ask for input about other aspects of middle school ministry.

twelve tribes of Israel. This may not have been the birthright and blessing Jacob had in mind, but it was ultimately all part of God's plan.

This Bible story will help your students see that nursing our wounds may keep us from seeing the big picture of what God is doing.

Take It to Your Students

Here are some key points to put in front of your students with this lesson:
- Think about how much you try to control things yourself.
- Keep your end of the deal instead of changing things to get your way.
- If something doesn't work out the way you planned, take a trust-step toward God. ✘

She Loves Me, She Loves Me Not: The Lesson

Take 1: Preview (15 to 20 minutes)

Setup: This activity will set up the day's Bible story in a relational way as students discover what would make each other's days perfect.

Props: Photocopies of "Perfect Day!" (p. 36), 1 per student; pens or pencils, supplies for the journal option you've chosen, markers
(*Optional: Shocking and Scandalous Stories from the Bible DVD,* TV and DVD player; smiley face stickers)

QUIET ON THE SET

To launch the lesson:
- Welcome everyone to the group. Use first names or preferred nicknames and introduce visitors. After your students have had some time to socialize, pull them in and have them get comfortable.
- Go over your Rules of Engagement if needed. (See the Rules of Engagement suggestions on p. 6 for more information.)
- Review the journaling component you've chosen for your group. (See Create a Group Journal on p. 10 for more information.)

2: She Loves Me, She Loves Me Not

ACTION

DVD Option: Start this activity by showing your group "Perfect Day!" from the *Shocking and Scandalous Stories from the Bible DVD* before students fill in their handouts.

Pass out pencils or pens and copies of the "Perfect Day!" handout, one per student. Prompt everybody to take a few minutes to fill in their handouts, then direct students to form pairs or trios to share their ideas of a perfect day.

> Nothing says "dull and boring" to middle schoolers like the silent roar of white noise during a supposedly fun activity. So set an upbeat tone by playing teen-friendly music in the background as students fill out their "Perfect Day!" handouts and share their answers with each other.

PLAY BACK

- **Ever have one of those days when everything seems to work?**

Spend some time letting students share some of those "perfect times" with each other.

Invite the group to vote in order to select their top 5 perfect days from everyone's sheets, then record the results in the group journal. If you've got smiley face stickers, have your students stick them on the group journal by the perfect day they each like best.

After the stickers are placed, show mock surprise and say: **Hold it, guys . . . the fine print in the Director's Guide says, "By order of the BDS (Bad Day Society) your Perfect Day has just been cancelled."** Sorry. Better luck next time.

> Have fun by creating a group video using this "Perfect Day!" activity. Just have one student at a time jump in front of the camera and call out one of the completed sentences from his or her sheet. Bring out the prop box and let teenagers dress up if they want. Keep things going at a snappy pace, with students jumping in from several directions. Play the video back later, perhaps for the entire church.

Wait for the *"How lame is this!"* groan, then have a volunteer use a marker to cross out the top 5 list from the journal and turn the smiley face stickers into frowns.

We had our hearts set on sharing some amazing times, didn't we?
Use these questions to get a group discussion going:

- **How do you usually handle disappointment? Give a real-life example.**
- **Fill in the blank:**
—**If disappointment were a color, its color would be _____.**
—**If disappointment were a taste, its taste would be _____.**

—If disappointment were a sound, its sound would be_____.
- Once we've been betrayed by somebody, we can easily lose our ability to trust that person. Has this ever happened to you? Why is betrayal so hard to shake off?

Happy surprises are wonderful. Unhappy surprises are much harder to bear. As you know, life is not always a check-the-box completion thing. Stuff happens to us that's contrary to the game plan. Today's Bible guy knows this all too well. *She Loves Me, She Love Me Not* is up next. ✘

Take 2: Feature Presentation (15 to 20 minutes)

Setup: Students will take a close look at the story of Jacob and Laban and discuss what it means to trust God even when things don't work out.

Props: Photocopies of **Outtakes** (p. 37); 4 or more large balloons, permanent markers

Optional: Bibles

QUIET ON THE SET

Pass out copies of **Outtakes**, one per student. *Optional:* Have students grab their own Bibles.

ACTION

Use **Outtakes** to introduce and teach the Bible story. First, briefly introduce the **Cast** and make sure your students know who's who. Next, use **Movie Trailer** to cover the highlights of the Bible background and story. Then read the Bible story (Genesis 29:15-28) out loud from **Outtakes** or have a volunteer read it. If you prefer, ask students to read the passage aloud from their own Bibles.

PLAY BACK

Ask volunteers to blow up four or more balloons and tie them closed. With a marker, label them "Jacob," "Laban," "Leah," and "Rachel." (Label additional balloons if you'll have more than two discussion teams.) Divide your group into two or more small teams for discussion with an adult or older teen leader for each group. If possible, plan to make the groups all guys or all girls. Guys

2: She Loves Me, She Loves Me Not

will explore the perspectives of Jacob and Laban (Guy Talk), while the girls look at things from Leah and Rachel's point of view (Girl Talk). If your group is small, you can discuss all the questions together, but choose discussion questions with sensitivity and aim to cover both the male and female perspectives on this story. Remind group leaders to be ready to enhance discussion with insights from **Why Is This PG-13 Story in the Bible?** (p. 27).

Have small groups discuss the questions and write key words from their answers on the balloons with permanent markers. Encourage everyone in each group to take a turn writing something.

Let's see if we can sort out what was going on inside the heads of the characters in this story. What were they *really* up to?

Guy Talk: Get into the heads of Jacob and Laban.

- **Do you think Laban had any hidden motives when he offered Jacob a job? Explain.** *(It's possible Laban had already seen Jacob's interest in his daughter.)*
- **What was Jacob hoping for when he made a deal with Laban? Would you have made a deal like that? Why or why not?**
- **What lessons did Jacob learn about being a real man, even though he was betrayed?** *(Even when things didn't go as he planned, he kept his end of the bargain. He thought about Rachel, not just himself.)*
- **What did Jacob have to trust God for?**

Girl Talk: Get into the heads of Leah and Rachel.

- **How do you think Leah and Rachel might have felt during the seven years of this story?** *(At the time, women had few rights, but that doesn't mean they didn't have emotions.)*
- **How were the women in this story deceived and betrayed? How would you have reacted if you were in their place? Why?**
- **If you were Leah, would you think Jacob did what was right? Why or why not?** *(Yes, because he didn't try to get rid of her.)*
- **How about if you were Rachel?** *(He kept his commitment to marry her even after he was tricked.)*
- **What did Leah and Rachel have to trust God for?**

Bring the discussion teams back together. Briefly review what they talked about by going over some of the things students wrote on the balloons.

Continue your discussion as a large group by asking questions like:
- **What do you think about the original bargain between Laban and Jacob?** *(It seems like a fair deal, but Laban may have had ulterior motives.)*
- **Considering Jacob's past, do you think he got what he deserved from Laban? Why or why not?** *(If you have not yet reviewed the Bible background, do this now to put Laban's deceit in the context of Jacob's story of deceit and betrayal.)*
- **How did Jacob's expectations fall apart? What do you think he felt or thought?**

Years earlier, Jacob grabbed control of his future by deceiving his older brother Esau and stealing his inheritance. But that didn't work out quite the way Jacob expected, did it? Jacob ended up experiencing betrayal for himself. But God had a plan: Jacob became the father of twelve sons, and his sons' families ended up forming the twelve tribes of Israel, God's chosen people. That's an inheritance Jacob could not have imagined for himself, even in his wildest dreams!

Ask the group questions like:
- **What are all the things that went wrong in Jacob's story?** *(Laban tricked Jacob. Jacob thought he would be finished in seven years but had to work fourteen. Rachel had to be the second wife rather than the first.)*
- **How did the things that went wrong become opportunities to trust God's plan?**
- **Why do you think this story about deception and betrayal is in the Bible?** *(This is a good time to remind students of the Bible verse: "And we know that in all things God works for the good of those who love him, who have been called according to his purpose" [Romans 8:28].)*

Ouch! Being blindsided by a deal-breaker is tough. Jacob's story certainly has a lot of lessons for us. One of the most important is that when things don't work out the way we expect, trust God's honest-to-goodness plan anyway. Just do it.

Take 3: Critics' Corner (15 to 20 minutes)

Setup: Reinforce the points you want your students to take away from today's lesson.
Props: Group journal with entries from Take 1; **Outtakes** (p. 37); large balloons, and a simple obstacle course using classroom furniture
(*Optional:* additional balloons, pennies)

2: She Loves Me, She Loves Me Not   33

QUIET ON THE SET

Grab the group journal and ask students to review their earlier entries describing a perfect day; together, compare and contrast them with Jacob's not-so-perfect day.

ACTION

Consider the POV

Ask the group:

- **Is there anything we can do when things don't work out the way we expect? Share your own ideas.**

Draw students' attention to the **POV** on the **Outtakes** handout: *When things don't work out the way you expect, trust God's plan anyway.* Invite them to describe what it looks like to trust God's plan in the middle of a disappointing situation.

Invite the group to talk about the upside to betrayal and disappointment. For example, we can learn to better empathize with others who've been hurt because we've experienced those feelings too.

Ask the group:

- **How does helping others keep our mind on positive things like God's grace?**

Jot down students' key insights in the group journal.

Understand God's Truth

Life is rarely predictable. Jacob expected to marry Rachel but got Leah instead. God still had a plan to give him Rachel. Who knew? God did.

Ask the group:

- **What have you learned from today's story? How does it speak to your life?**
(Trust God's plan. Don't hold new experiences captive to the disappointments of the past.)

Who doesn't daydream about future loves, lives, and careers? But when things don't work out how we hoped, we can stop, take a breath, and trust that the creator has a plan.

Teamwork

Remember, in life, as on the sports field, endurance is often the name of the game. Let's be there for each other this week as we face unexpected challenges. Let's lean on each other for prayer and support.

PLAY BACK

Wrap up the meeting with a team-building game in which students work together to overcome challenges. Then close in prayer.

I've Got Your Back

Needed: balloons, basket, simple obstacle course; additional balloons and pennies for the closing prayer experience

Goal: Pair up to get air-filled balloons through an obstacle course and into a basket.

How to Play:

You can set up an easy obstacle course in advance or invite students to help design and put it together on the spot—just use common classroom furniture like chairs, bean bags, tables, and so on. Have teenagers blow up balloons; you'll need one balloon for every two players. Direct students to pair up and stand back-to-back. Place a balloon between the backs of the paired players, right above the waistline.

Explain that the object of this game is for pairs to negotiate their way through the obstacle course without dropping their balloons. Elbows cannot be used to secure balloons, but each pair can have *one* chance to use their hands to adjust balloons during play. If a team drops their balloon, they need to go back to the start of the obstacle course and start over. This activity is all about working together toward a common goal (with some disappointment along the way!).

After the game, compliment students on their teamwork as they helped each other make it through, over, under, and around the various obstacles and challenges in their way. Then say: **Life isn't fair. You'll have to do doggie duty, and your sister won't! Your friend will make the team, and you'll get cut. You'll get stuck with pimples and braces when your best friend looks like a supermodel.**

We'll each face huge disappointments and hurts. But God's specialty is to weave all the tattered pieces of our lives into something extraordinarily good. Trust it to happen for you.

Close with Prayer

Ask your group to look again at **Outtakes** and repeat today's **Key Verse**: "And we know that in all things God works for the good of those who love him, who have been called according to his purpose" (Romans 8:28). Then point out this week's *Verse-atility*, a personalized wording of the Key Verse: *God works all the parts of my life into something good.* If you've got enough time, have a volunteer write the verse in your group journal and invite everybody to initial it.

> Help your students discover that prayer can take many forms beyond the traditional "fold your hands, close your eyes, and bow your head" approach. Music, art, physical posture, hands-on experiences and expressions—these can all be part of prayer. Whenever you can, seize the opportunity to help your group engage with God in a variety of experiential ways.

Invite students to share prayer requests, especially about challenges or unexpected disappointments they're facing. For each request shared, have a different volunteer grab a balloon and a penny; they should insert the penny into the balloon, then fill the balloon with air and tie it closed. When all the requests are shared, lead the group in a unique sensory prayer experience. Prompt everyone to shake their balloons and roll the pennies around while you pray, the sounds signifying each request that's being lifted up to God. ✘

> **Verse-atility:** *God works all the parts of my life into something good.*

Perfect Day!

INSTRUCTIONS:
Fill in your Perfect Day! sheet. Be sure to come up with "cool points" for each entry for a total of a Perfect 100 score. When you're done, get together with a friend or two and share your answers with each other.

(Name)_____ is about to have the most Perfectly Awesome Day!

My perfect day begins with . . . _____
_____
_____ (Cool points: _____)

My perfect day ends with . . . _____
_____
_____ (Cool points: _____)

My perfect day would include spending time with these amazing people: _____
_____
_____ (Cool points: _____)

My perfect day would include a visit to this awesome place: _____
_____
_____ (Cool points: _____)

My perfect day would include snuggling with my pet: _____
_____ (Cool points: _____)

My perfect day would include eating this incredible edible: _____
_____ (Cool points: _____)

My perfect day means absolutely, positively not having to do these three things:
1) _____
2) _____
3) _____ (Cool points: _____)

My perfect day could not be awesomely perfect without this: _____
_____
_____ (Cool points: _____)

Total: 100 points!

Permission is granted by Standard Publishing to reproduce "Perfect Day!" for ministry purposes only (not for resale).

Outtakes

CAST

Jacob: tricked his father into blessing him instead of his older brother
Laban: Jacob's uncle, who has two daughters to marry off and tricks Jacob
Leah: the older daughter
Rachel: the younger, beautiful daughter

MOVIE TRAILER

- Jacob flees his homeland after tricking his father into blessing him.
- Jacob works seven years for his uncle, Laban, so he can marry Rachel.
- At the wedding, Laban tricks Jacob and gives him Leah instead.
- After the wedding night, Jacob discovers what happened and confronts Laban.
- Laban has Jacob over a barrel because Jacob is still in love with Rachel.
- Jacob marries Rachel and works another seven years for Laban.

Verse-atility: God works all the parts of my life into something good.

POV: When things don't work out the way you expect, trust God's plan anyway.

Key Verse: And we know that in all things God works for the good of those who love him, who have been called according to his purpose (Romans 8:28).

SHE LOVES ME, SHE LOVES ME NOT

Genesis 29:15-28 *(The Message)*
(We've added a few of our own comments **in bold** *below.)*

[The back story: Jacob tricked his father into giving him the blessing his brother Esau should have gotten, so Jacob had to run for his life. He went to live with his uncle, Laban.]

When Jacob had been with him for a month, Laban said, "Just because you're my nephew, you shouldn't work for me for nothing. Tell me what you want to be paid. What's a fair wage?"

Now Laban had two daughters; Leah was the older and Rachel the younger. Leah had nice eyes, but Rachel was stunningly beautiful. And it was Rachel that Jacob loved.

So Jacob answered, "I will work for you seven years for your younger daughter Rachel." **[True love.]**

"It is far better," said Laban, "that I give her to you than marry her to some outsider. Yes. Stay here with me." So Jacob worked seven years for Rachel. But it only seemed like a few days, he loved her so much.

Then Jacob said to Laban, "Give me my wife; I've completed what we agreed I'd do. I'm ready to consummate my marriage." **[In other words: have sex.]** Laban invited everyone around and threw a big feast. At evening, though, he got his daughter Leah and brought her to the marriage bed, and Jacob slept with her. (Laban gave his maid Zilpah to his daughter Leah as her maid.)

Morning came: There was Leah in the marriage bed! **[Oh, brother . . .]**

Jacob confronted Laban, "What have you done to me? Didn't I work all this time for the hand of Rachel? Why did you cheat me?"

"We don't do it that way in our country," said Laban. "We don't marry off the younger daughter before the older. Enjoy your week of honeymoon, and then we'll give you the other one also. But it will cost you another seven years of work." **[Stick with it, Jacob!]**

Jacob agreed. When he'd completed the honeymoon week, Laban gave him his daughter Rachel to be his wife.

Permission is granted by Standard Publishing to reproduce this **Outtakes** handout for ministry purposes only (not for resale).

3

Gangland

Director's Commentary

NOW SHOWING: *Gangland*

FROM THE BIBLE: Korah leads a rebellion against Moses (Numbers 16:1-3, 16-21, 28-32, 35).

RATED PG-13 FOR: dissension, rebellion, human incineration, and treating God with contempt

POV: Discover God's purpose for you rather than wanting what he gives others.

KEY VERSE: "For it is God who works in you to will and to act according to his good purpose" (Philippians 2:13).

The Lesson	Time	What you'll do . . .	How you'll do it . . .	What you'll need . . .
Take 1: Preview	15 to 20 minutes	Start off your lesson by introducing the theme with a relational, creative activity.	Option 1: Students create unique pieces of art.	Magazines (or other soft writing surfaces), blank paper, pens or pencils, colorful markers; 1 photocopy of "I've Got To Be Me" handout (pp. 48, 49); group journal supplies (*Optional:* CD player, CD of upbeat music)
			Option 2: Students watch a DVD version of "Unique" and discuss it. Or, choose to do both.	*Shocking and Scandalous Stories from the Bible* DVD, TV and DVD player
Take 2: Feature Presentation	15 to 20 minutes	Dive into the Bible story and explore it together.	Small group and large group discussion	Photocopies of **Outtakes** (p. 50); pieces of poster board, markers *Optional:* Bibles
Take 3: Critics' Corner	15 to 20 minutes	Help your students grasp God's point of view and wrap things up with a fun team-building activity.	Discussion, game, and prayer	Photocopies of **Outtakes** (p. 50); group journal; plastic grocery store bags (1 per student), 1 large box, lots of Styrofoam packing peanuts

3: Gangland

WHY IS THIS PG-13 STORY IN THE BIBLE?

Moses is no stranger to rebellion—he'd shown a rebellious streak of his own in his younger days, murdering an Egyptian and running for his life when his crime was discovered. Later, after God called him back to lead the Israelites out of slavery in Egypt, Moses endured the betrayal of his own brother, Aaron, who sculpted a golden calf to worship while Moses was busy getting the Ten Commandments from the one true God.

Now their cousin Korah is up to no good (their fathers were brothers—see Exodus 6:18-21). He wants to know why Moses and Aaron get all the fame and power. So Korah rounds up 250 others and incites a mob.

Korah is no slouch to begin with. Because he's a Levite, Korah has daily responsibilities in the Tent of Meeting, the center of Israel's worship. In fact, all the 250 guys he convinces to see things his way are leaders as well. But there's his cousin Moses calling all the shots. Korah claims the whole community is holy and Moses is not really the boss of anything.

Moses has been through plenty of challenges by now, and he's not particularly afraid that God is looking to replace him. He invites all the rebels to meet at the Tent of Meeting and lets God clarify things. Moses doesn't say a word in his own defense. While Korah makes a play for fame and power, Moses simply wants what God wants.

God shows up at the Tent of Meeting. Moses leaves the whole mess in God's hands; he announces that if God wants him to continue leading Israel, the earth will open up and swallow the rebel leaders right there in the sight of the people. And that's exactly what happens. Then fire from God consumes the rest of the rebels. The message is clear.

This Bible story will show your students that satisfaction does not come from arrogantly grabbing for power and fame, but in being what God wants you to be.

Take It to Your Students

Here are some key points to put in front of your students with this lesson:

Connecting with Community
Log on to www.shockingandscandalous.com to connect with other ministries:
- Check out a sample video of other students in action.
- Share with other leaders at the PG-13 forum about what's working in your ministry, what's not, or how you used *Shocking and Scandalous* this week.
- Or ask for input about other aspects of middle school ministry.

SHOCKING AND SCANDALOUS STORIES FROM THE BIBLE

- Grabbing for something that's not yours isn't the way to go.
- God cares about your attitude as you serve him.
- Look for God's purpose for you rather than worrying about what others have. ✗

Gangland: The Lesson

Take 1: Preview (15 to 20 minutes)

Setup: This activity will set up the day's Bible story in a relational way as students zero in on what makes them unique.

Props: A somewhat soft writing surface for students (like magazines to put under their papers), 1 photocopy of the "I've Got to Be Me" handout (pp. 48, 49), blank paper, sharpened pencils, a variety of colorful markers, and supplies for the journal option you've chosen

(*Optional:* CD player and upbeat music to play in the background while students make their name artwork)

QUIET ON THE SET

To launch this lesson:
- Welcome everyone to the group. Use first names or preferred nicknames and introduce visitors. After your students have had some time to socialize, pull them in and have them get comfortable.
- Go over your Rules of Engagement if needed. (See the Rules of Engagement suggestions on p. 6 for more information.)
- Review the journaling component you've chosen for your group. (See the Create a Group Journal section on p. 10 for more information.)

ACTION

Lead the group in making unique pieces of art that feature each student's name. To do so, invite everybody to grab a magazine (to serve as a writing surface), a plain sheet of paper, a sharpened pencil, and a few colored markers. Direct everyone to fold their plain paper in half lengthwise and press the crease firmly. Then, using the magazines as placemats, ask students to write their first names in a large, cursive style along the creased edge of their paper. (For the activity to work, the surface *must* be soft, and you must press very firmly; pen is better than pencil.) Have students open their papers; a light mirror impression of their name will appear opposite the original. Prompt students to take a few minutes to retrace both impressions with bright, bold color, creating their own design and adding other decorations to the picture if they'd like. It might look something like this:

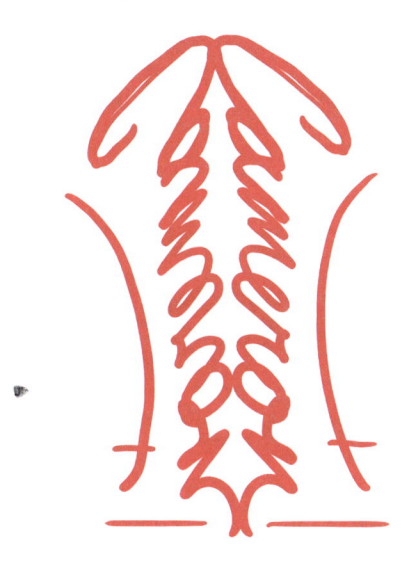

PLAY BACK

Invite students to hold up their finished drawings and spend some time as a group admiring each other's name artwork. Emphasize that each piece of art is unique—no two are alike. Explain that, like the artwork, God has a unique purpose for each person in your group and it's their job to discover what that purpose is.

Have a volunteer cut apart the six boxes on the "I've Got to Be Me" handout (pp. 48, 49) and tape the pieces to the group journal. Read them each aloud, then use checkmarks to record how many students personally relate to each of the scenarios. Give students the opportunity to comment or edit scenarios, sharing how they connect with the various personalities described and also some specific ways that they'd describe themselves differently.

> Some of your students may say they don't relate to any of the examples. If that's the case, ask those students to simply choose the one that comes *closest* to their own personality.

Encourage all students to participate with the journal, even if it is just to initial in agreement.

Who are you? God knows. And he wants you to discover your own comfortable space in the world—without having to feel hounded to be someone you're not.

DVD Option: Kick-start the following discussion below by first showing "Unique" from the *Shocking and Scandalous Stories from the Bible DVD*.

Help your students discover the truth that no two people in your group are completely alike by having them mingle as they share their answers to the following questions. To do so, have students find partners and share answers to the first question; then ask them to find a new partner each time you ask a new question.

Ask your group:
- What's one thing you're really good at?
- If you could go on a trip anywhere in the world, where would you want to go? Why?
- What is something that makes you really, really happy?
- Imagine a perfect world built just for you. What's one thing you'd want the most in that perfect world?
- We're like our friends, but we're different too. What do you think it means to be "unique"? Explain.

God has something in store for *you*. When we ignore his unique purpose for each of us, we tend to grab hold of things that are not a good fit. The result? We're not easy to live with; we're crabby and rebellious.

Up next: On location, we'll meet a greedy, grubby ensemble grab-happy for power and fame. The earth splits. Lightning strikes twice. Cataclysm in process . . . in *Gangland*, straight ahead. ✖

Take 2: Feature Presentation (15 to 20 minutes)

Setup: Students will take a close look at the story of Korah's rebellion and discuss finding God's purpose for them.

Props: Photocopies of **Outtakes** (p. 50); pieces of poster board (or newsprint), markers

Optional: Bibles

3: Gangland 43

QUIET ON THE SET

Pass out copies of **Outtakes**, one per student. *Optional:* Have students grab their own Bibles.

ACTION

Use **Outtakes** to introduce and teach the Bible story. First, briefly introduce the **Cast** and make sure your students know who's who. Next, use the **Movie Trailer** to cover the highlights of the Bible background and story. Then read the Bible story (Numbers 16:1-3, 16-21, 28-32, 35) out loud from **Outtakes** or have volunteers read it. If you prefer, ask students to read the passages aloud from their own Bibles.

PLAY BACK

Divide your group into two or more small teams for discussion with an adult or older teen leader for each group. Assign half of the groups to explore the point of view of Korah and his followers (Team Talk 1) and have the remaining groups look at things from the perspective of Moses and Aaron (Team Talk 2).

Give each small group a piece of poster board (or sheet of newsprint) and markers. Ask each group to write the letters L-E-A-D-E-R on their poster and explain that they should use these letters to take notes on their answers to the discussion questions, creating a word or short sentence around each letter. They can answer any question beginning with any letter or answer the same question with more than one letter. Remind group leaders to be ready to enhance their team's discussion with insights from **Why Is This PG-13 Story in the Bible?** (p. 39).

Let's take it inside out. Since Korah thought the issue was who should be the leader, answer these questions with words or phrases that start with the letters in "leader."

Team Talk 1: Get into the heads of Korah and his followers.

- **What reason did Korah give for not wanting to follow Moses' lead? Do you think that was the real reason? Why or why not?** *(All the people were equally holy.)*
- **Why do you think Korah rounded up rebels to go with him to confront Moses?** *(Deceived into thinking there is power in numbers.)*
- **Why would the other rebel leaders take Korah's side?** *(Each wants to be important.)*
- **How would you describe Korah's character?**

SHOCKING AND SCANDALOUS STORIES FROM THE BIBLE

Team Talk 2: Get into the heads of Moses and Aaron.

> Consider making a video of your students answering one or more of these questions. Play it back later.

- **What do you know about Moses' and Aaron's lives before this story? What did they do? What were they like?** *(Amazing stuff: Moses in a basket as a baby; burning bush; showdown with Pharaoh; Red Sea crossing; Ten Commandments; golden calf idol)*
- **How do Moses and Aaron handle the rebels in this story? Why do you think they handle things that way?** *(Let God decide things.)*
- **How do Moses and Aaron get out of the way and let God deal with the problem?** *(Don't defend themselves, but ask God what to do and follow instructions.)*
- **How would you describe Moses' character?**

Bring the discussion teams back together. Briefly review results of their discussions by inviting volunteers to share what they wrote on their "LEADER" posters. Continue your discussion as a large group by asking questions like:

- **What do you think about Korah's claim that the whole community was holy? Was he right or wrong?** *(Yes, the Israelites were God's chosen people, but clearly God had chosen Moses to lead.)*
- **How did Korah show what was in his heart?**
- **How did Moses show what was in his heart?**
- **Why do you think this story about jealousy and rebellion is in the Bible?** *(This is a good opportunity to remind students of the Bible verse: "For it is God who works in you to will and to act according to his good purpose" [Philippians 2:13].)*

God knew what Korah was really up to. Korah was thinking of what he wanted for himself (greedy, grubby, grab!)—not about what God wanted for him or for all the Israelites.

Use these questions to kick off more large-group discussion:

- **Where in this story could Korah have changed course and stopped the rebellion?**
- **What happened because he chose to continue in rebellion?** *(The rebels were killed, but all the people saw that God really had chosen Moses.)*
- **How does today's Key Verse (Philippians 2:13) connect to the Bible story?**

3: Gangland

We can make the same mistake Korah made when we crave what God gives to others. God created each of us differently—you know that—and has a future planned that's unique to you. Discover God's purpose for you rather than grabbing after what he gives others. ✘

Take 3: Critics' Corner (15 to 20 minutes)

Setup: Reinforce the points you want your students to take away from today's lesson.
Props: Group journal with entries from Take 1; **Outtakes** (p. 50); plastic grocery store bags (1 per student), and a large box filled with foam packing peanuts

QUIET ON THE SET

Grab the group journal and lead the group in reviewing what they've discussed and jotted down so far. Use this quick review to remind your students to see themselves as God does: amazingly unique.

ACTION

Consider the POV

Ask:
- **What happens when you try to be someone you're not?**
- **Have you ever experienced this in your own life? Explain.**

Discuss God's purpose for your group: helping one another seek God's will. God's purpose is higher and brighter than today's individualistic "looks and money" culture.

Reinforce the **POV** on the **Outtakes** handout: *Discover God's purpose for you rather than wanting what he gives others.*

Invite the students to join you in repeating today's Key Verse out loud: "For it is God who works in you to will and to act according to his good purpose" (Philippians 2:13).

Understand God's Truth

Feeling good about ourselves does not come from being bossy or conceited or trying to muscle in on other people's star power. Want to be a leader like Moses? Practice the hard stuff. Practice responsibility over rebellion.

> Introverted teens and preteens will open up more when they're in a safe conversation with a friend. If you want, have students form pairs to discuss the final question ("What is the toughest part of being satisfied with who you are?").

Ask the group:

- **What have we learned from today's story?** *(God's authority rules over wealth and influence. Trying to be what you're not doesn't end well.)*
- **How can greed affect our common sense? Share some examples.**
- **What is the toughest part of being satisfied with who you are?**

In today's story, God is involved. He's present. And he acts powerfully. Moses, who is not seeking power or fame, leans heavily on God's authority. In other words, craving what others have is a pretty big time waster.

Teamwork

Invite the group to brainstorm some specific ideas in response to these questions:

- How can we help each other be content with who God made us to be?
- How can we help each other discover God's purpose for our lives?

Remind the group of the power of teamwork: They can make a huge difference in each other's lives by encouraging and praying for each other.

PLAY BACK

Wrap up the meeting with a light-hearted game that helps participants reflect on their own unique interests and talents. Then close in prayer.

Pop Culture Grab!

Needed: plastic grocery store bags (1 per student) and a large box filled with Styrofoam (packing) peanuts

Goal: Work together to try to fill bags with foam peanuts.

How to Play:

Distribute plastic grocery bags, one per player. Ask students to hold bags by their handles. Set a large box of foam peanuts on a table or the floor and gather your group around it. Tell students that the peanuts represent talents and gifts that they might want to possess. Talk about real-life examples, such as "I wish I had a great singing voice like Taylor Swift," or "I wish I were a star

3: Gangland

athlete like Kobe," or "I wish I was the best gamer that ever lived," and so on. On the count of three, have students fill their bags with as many "talents" (peanuts) as possible. Your group will find out that it is almost impossible to get the peanuts to stay in their bags! Most will pop out of the bag and stick to hands and arms due to static electricity.

> There's nothing like the power of laughter to build and strengthen relationships. Enjoy the silliness of this game! When your students have fun with one another, it serves as a powerful glue that helps them bond together.

After the game, say: **Trust God's blueprint. There's no one like you. You're here to embrace *your* gifts and skills and unique personalities. Take confidence and discover who you are—not who you're not. Keep digging. Discover God's purpose in you!**

Close with Prayer

Ask your group to look again at **Outtakes** and repeat today's **Key Verse:** "For it is God who works in you to will and to act according to his good purpose" (Philippians 2:13). Then point out this week's *Verse-atility: God in me: He helps me do things his way.* If time permits, jot the verse in the group journal and have everyone initial it. Encourage your students to try to keep God's truth front and center in their lives this week.

> **Verse-atility:** *God in me: He helps me do things his way.*

Invite students to spend some time quietly praying, inviting God to guide each of them in the unique purpose he has for them. Then ask students to share any prayer requests. Lead the group in praying for the requests, then ask God to give each student the strength to be confident in God's love and guidance in their own lives. ✘

I've Got to Be Me

The Nature Lover
I love the outdoors. Camping, hiking, the ocean. I want to be a marine biologist when I grow up. Creepy-crawlies don't bother me at all. I'll save a fly from a swatter if I can just get to it first!

The Decorator
I'm a frustrated interior designer! My bedroom walls are lime green. But deep purple is my fave. Pillows, curtains, plants, photo frames, diaries, and scrapbooks all need to match. Oh, and I'm Volunteer #1 when the school drama club needs new sets.

Kids-R-ME
I'm poetry in motion on a skateboard (no kidding, you should see me!), but I like kids too. I'll make snacks or practice guitar for a song they like and then rush to the gym to work out and shoot hoops. Crazy, but that's me!

Big Biz

When I was little I had a lemonade stand. I really got into having my own business. I made the lemonade and the fliers and even made deliveries—right to the car windows! Someday I want to run my own sports drink company.

Whiz Kid

I actually enjoy doing homework—and I'm not ashamed to admit it! School is my thing. I like most of my classes and I love learning new things. Sure, some teachers can be boring, but for the most part, school's something that just clicks with me. I'm looking forward to high school, then college, then who knows what.

The Sport

Basketball, tennis, soccer, you name it—I like to play it. I'm happiest when I'm doing something active, like playing a pick-up game with friends, working out with my team after school, or going for a weekend run. I'm not sure what I want to do career-wise in the future, but I know I'll be into sports for the rest of my life.

Permission is granted by Standard Publishing to reproduce "I've Got to Be Me" for ministry purposes only (not for resale).

Outtakes

CAST
Korah: a leader in the Tent of Meeting who starts a rebellion against Moses
Dathan, Abiran, and On: leaders from the tribe of Reuben who join Korah's rebellion
Moses: God's chosen leader for the people of Israel
Aaron: Moses' brother and assistant leader

MOVIE TRAILER
- Korah decides he doesn't like Moses' leadership.
- Korah rounds up 250 other rebel leaders to confront Moses with him.
- Moses tells Korah to come before God with him and let God decide who should lead.
- The glory of God appears at the Tent of Meeting for everyone to see.
- God chooses Moses to remain as leader.
- The earth opens up and swallows the rebel leaders; fire from God burns up the rest of the rebels.

Verse-atility: God in me: He helps me do things his way.

POV: Discover God's purpose for you rather than wanting what he gives others.

Key Verse: For it is God who works in you to will and to act according to his good purpose (Philippians 2:13).

GANGLAND
Numbers 16:1-3, 16-21, 28-32, 35 *(The Message)*
*(We've added a few of our own comments **in bold** below.)*

Getting on his high horse one day, Korah son of Izhar, the son of Kohath, the son of Levi, along with a few Reubenites—Dathan and Abiram sons of Eliab, and On son of Peleth—rebelled against Moses. He had with him 250 leaders of the congregation of Israel, prominent men with positions in the Council. They came as a group **[a gang is more like it]** and confronted Moses and Aaron, saying, "You've overstepped yourself. This entire community is holy and God is in their midst. So why do you act like you're running the whole show?" **[Who does "Big K" think he is?]**

. . . Moses said to Korah, "Bring your people before God tomorrow. Appear there with them and Aaron. Have each man bring his censer filled with incense and present it to God—all 250 censers. And you and Aaron do the same, bring your censers."

So they all did it. They brought their censers filled with fire and incense and stood at the entrance of the Tent of Meeting. Moses and Aaron did the same.

It was Korah and his gang against Moses and Aaron at the entrance of the Tent of Meeting. **[A tense moment!]** The entire community could see the Glory of God.

God said to Moses and Aaron, "Separate yourselves from this congregation so that I can finish them off and be done with them."

. . . Moses continued to address the community: "This is how you'll know that it was God who sent me to do all these things and that it wasn't anything I cooked up on my own. If these men die a natural death like all the rest of us, you'll know that it wasn't God who sent me. But if God does something unprecedented—if the ground opens up and swallows the lot of them and they are pitched alive into Sheol **[the dead zone]**—then you'll know that these men have been insolent with God."

The words were hardly out of his mouth when the Earth split open. Earth opened its mouth and in one gulp swallowed them down, the men and their families, all the human beings connected with Korah, along with everything they owned. . . .

Then God sent lightning. The fire cremated the 250 men who were offering the incense. **[Wow . . .]**

Permission is granted by Standard Publishing to reproduce this **Outtakes** handout for ministry purposes only (not for resale).

4 Earth Angel

Director's Commentary

NOW SHOWING: *Earth Angel*

FROM THE BIBLE: Rahab protects the Israelite spies (Joshua 2:1-15).

RATED PG-13 FOR: references to sexual immorality, deceit

POV: We're not perfect—but God is approachable. Our commitment to him makes a difference.

KEY VERSE: "Being confident of this, that he who began a good work in you will carry it on to completion until the day of Christ Jesus" (Philippians 1:6).

The Lesson	Time	What you'll do . . .	How you'll do it . . .	What you'll need . . .
Take 1: Preview	15 to 20 minutes	Start off your lesson by introducing the theme with a relational, creative activity.	Option 1: Students solve word puzzles and discuss connections between friends.	Dry-erase board and dry-erase markers, eraser; group journal supplies (*Optional:* game show set supplies, game show host costume)
			Option 2: Students watch a DVD version of "Connected" and discuss it. Or, choose to do both.	*Shocking and Scandalous Stories from the Bible DVD*, TV and DVD player
Take 2: Feature Presentation	15 to 20 minutes	Dive into the Bible story and explore it together.	Small group and large group discussion	Photocopies of **Outtakes** (p. 62); construction paper, scissors, markers (*Optional:* Bibles, pieces of poster board or foam core)
Take 3: Critics' Corner	15 to 20 minutes	Help your students grasp God's point of view and wrap things up with a fun team-building activity.	Discussion, game, and prayer	Photocopies of **Outtakes** (p. 62); group journal; lots of plastic or foam beverage cups, masking or duct tape

SHOCKING AND SCANDALOUS STORIES FROM THE BIBLE

Why Is This PG-13 Story in the Bible?

A couple of upright Hebrew men are trying to look inconspicuous in a foreign city. So where do they go? To a prostitute's house, of course. Josephus the historian calls Rahab an "innkeeper." Visitors to her house, which was built into the wall around Jericho, were probably offered both a place to stay and sexual favors. The two spies could have gone there intentionally hoping to be mistaken as customers. The location of Rahab's home, right on the wall, would also give them a quick exit if they needed it—which they did.

The reputation of the Israelites and their God has gone ahead of the spies. Although they try to be discrete, the king of Jericho knows the spies are in his city. He even knows they are at Rahab's house. So why shouldn't Rahab just hand them over? Doesn't she have more to gain by pleasing her own king than by protecting foreign spies?

Rahab has heard stories about the Israelites. She knows about the miraculous crossing of the Red Sea when they left Egypt forty years earlier. She knows the Israelite army has already stormed through several other cities. She knows God is giving the land to this people. Because of all this, she chooses to ally herself with the spies. Instead of handing the spies over to the king, she sends the king's messengers on a wild goose chase, hides the spies, and sneaks them safely out of the city. In exchange, she asks to be spared in the coming battle.

Rahab flat-out lies for the spies. We could go in circles about whether a lie like this is justified and whether God condones lying in some situations; it's a question philosophers and theologians have wrestled with for centuries. Could she have said something else and still saved the spies? We don't know. But what we know for sure is that Rahab made a decision under pressure when lives were at stake. The bigger issue here is that God asks us to trust him—and Rahab does just that. The New Testament recognizes and honors her for faith (see Hebrews 11:31 and James 2:25) and, as it turns out, Rahab is actually an ancestor of Jesus (Matthew 1:5)!

Connecting with Community
Log on to www.shockingandscandalous.com to connect with other ministries:
- Check out a sample video of other students in action.
- Share with other leaders at the PG-13 forum about what's working in your ministry, what's not, or how you used *Shocking and Scandalous* this week.
- Or ask for input about other aspects of middle school ministry.

4: Earth Angel

In Rahab's story we see how God used an unlikely combination of human interactions and an even more unlikely hero—a prostitute—to set up the events that gave his people a new land and eventually gave the world a Savior. This Bible story will help middle schoolers recognize that God often works in unexpected ways; we should keep our hearts and minds open.

Take It to Your Students

Here are some key points to put in front of your students with this lesson:
- **God is at work in the world, even through sinners like you and me.**
- **No matter the situation, trusting God is the top choice.**
- **We're not perfect, but God accepts sinners who do his will.** ✘

Earth Angel: The Lesson

Take 1: Preview   (15 to 20 minutes)

Setup: This activity will set up the day's Bible story in a relational way as students participate in a game show highlighting the ways friends help them feel connected.

Set design: If you want, create a game show set in your room with a large "Wheel of Fortune"-style board, podiums for players, a game show host costume, and so on. Hang up a large banner that says "2 Good 2 Be 4-Gotten."

Props: A dry-erase board, dry-erase markers, and eraser; group journal supplies and markers

QUIET ON THE SET

To launch the lesson:
- Welcome everyone to the group. Use first names or preferred nicknames and introduce visitors. After your students have had some time to socialize, pull them in and have them get comfortable.
- Go over your Rules of Engagement, if needed. (See the Rules of Engagement suggestions on p. 6 for more information.)

- Review the journaling component you've chosen for your group. (See Create a Group Journal on p. 10 for more information.)

ACTION

Create a game show atmosphere for this Take 1 activity. Props can be simple or elaborate, depending on your setting. You can set up a "Wheel of Fortune"-style board, a place for players to stand, and a place for the game show host (you!) to stand. If you want, wear some cheesy game-show-host clothes and use your best game-show-host voice to lead the game. Use a computer and projector if you wish. Or, for the simplest version of this game, simply use a dry-erase board and markers.

Welcome students to the game show called "2 Good 2 Be 4-Gotten." To play, use the phrases below to create a "Wheel of Fortune"-style guessing game. Divide your group into two or more teams and have them work together to play. Start by writing blank lines to represent each letter in a given phrase. Have teams take turns guessing letters; as they do, write the correct ones in the appropriate blanks. Whenever a team guesses a letter that is part of the answer, give them a chance to guess what the answer is.

Use the following phrases to play five rounds of the game:

good laughs   good advice
good prayers   good gifts
good times

Once all five puzzles have been solved, lead a bonus round with the following puzzle (including both letters and blanks):

"_ _ _ r l_ _ e, _ L _r_, re_ _ _ es t_ t_e _e_ _ens,
         _ _ _r _ _ _t _ _ _ lness t_ t_e s_ _ es."

Say: **Let's solve this puzzle to see why our God is 2 Good 2 Be 4-Gotten! We'll get started with these common letters: e, r, s, t, l, n.**

Lead teams in guessing letters until they discover the answer, which is the text of Psalm 36:5—**"Your love, O Lord, reaches to the heavens, your faithfulness to the skies."**

4: Earth Angel

PLAY BACK

Invite a volunteer to write "2 Good 2 Be 4-Gotten" in your group journal with today's date. Ask the volunteer to record the five puzzle answers, then invite everybody to raise a hand and use their fingers to rate each of the puzzle answers on a "connect-ability" scale of 1 to 5 (1 meaning that it doesn't do much to help them deeply connect with a friend and 5 meaning it goes a long way in deepening their sense of connection with a friend). Total the score given to each answer and write it in the journal. Then lead the group in reviewing how they scored the answers, inviting students to share their reasoning for giving any especially high or especially low ratings.

Spend some time discussing how friends keep us connected and help us feel good about ourselves, and add any new "connect-ability" insights to your group journal.

We want to feel connected. We want to fit in. The social world is an important part of who we are.

DVD Option: Kick-start the discussion below by first showing "Connected" from the *Shocking and Scandalous Stories from the Bible DVD*.

Then use these questions—some of them from the DVD, with more added for your group—to get discussion going among your students:

- What sorts of things help you feel connected with your friends?
- When we're connected with our friends, it helps us feel wanted and secure. When have you felt this way?
- Think of a time you were disconnected—when you didn't have close friendships or when those friendships weren't going so well. What was it like? How did you feel? *(Hurt, left out, unwanted, lonely)*
- Have you ever noticed someone who wasn't connected—who didn't have close friends? Have you tried to connect with somebody like that? What happened?
- Why do you think people mistreat others who are social outsiders?
- What's tough about accepting or connecting with people who are different from you?

The female star in today's screening stands apart. She was a big-time sinner and a social misfit. Yet she risks everything for a God she barely knows. Meet this imperfect, unexpected hero for the faith in *Earth Angel*, up next. ✘

Take 2: Feature Presentation (15 to 20 minutes)

Setup: Your students will take a close look at the story of Rahab and the spies and discuss what God can do—even through people who make mistakes.

Props: Photocopies of **Outtakes** (p. 62); construction paper, scissors, markers, tape (*Optional:* Bibles, pieces of poster board or foam core)

QUIET ON THE SET

Pass out copies of **Outtakes**, one per student. (*Optional:* Have students grab their own Bibles; pieces of posterboard or foam core)

ACTION

Use **Outtakes** to introduce and teach the Bible story. First, briefly introduce the **Cast** and make sure your students know who's who. Next, use **Movie Trailer** to cover the highlights of the Bible background and story. Then read the Bible story (Joshua 2:1-15) out loud from **Outtakes** or have a volunteer read it. If you prefer, ask students to read from their own Bibles.

> As students write on their construction paper houses, let them know that they don't have to write down every answer. Also, rather than writing words, some students might want to draw faces or symbols that express emotions or thoughts.

PLAY BACK

Divide your group into two or more small teams for discussion with an adult or older teen leader for each group. If possible, plan to make the groups all guys or all girls. The guys will look at things from the point of view of the spies (Guy Talk); the girls will explore Rahab's perspective (Girl Talk). Remind group leaders to be ready to enhance the discussion with insights from **Why Is This PG-13 Story in the Bible?** (p. 52).

Give every group a pile of construction paper, scissors, and markers. Say: **Rahab's house was part of the wall surrounding Jericho. Cut a sheet of paper into the shape of a house, then write your thoughts on your house about the questions your group discusses.**

Guy Talk: Get into the heads of the spies.

- **How were the spies people who didn't fit in?** *(They were in a foreign land on a secret mission.)*

4: Earth Angel

- **What do you think was running through their heads when the king's messengers arrived?** *(Danger! Try to trust God.)*
- **Do you think they ever expected to have to depend on someone like Rahab—a woman who sold her body for money? Explain.** *(They probably thought they had everything under control. A prostitute—or any woman—would be the last person they turned to for help.)*
- **The spies agreed to Rahab's request. How do you think they viewed Rahab at this point?** *(They were all on the same side now. They were all trying to do God's will in a tough situation.)*

Girl Talk: Get into the head of Rahab.

- **How was Rahab a person who didn't fit in?** *(She sold sex for money.)*
- **What did Rahab have to be afraid of?** *(The community's scorn; possibly the spies; the king's messengers; the coming battle against Israel)*
- **How might being a woman make Rahab vulnerable?** *(She wasn't a soldier. She wasn't trained to fight like a soldier. She had to depend on others to look out for her.)*
- **What do you think made Rahab decide to hide the spies rather than just hand them over?** *(She believed in the one true God and wanted to be on his side.)*

Bring the groups back together. Briefly review results of discussions by having students attach their houses to a wall (or onto pieces of poster board or foam core). Butt the houses up against each other to form a city wall. Go over some of the words, phrases, or symbols students have written on their houses, inviting the group to comment on what they talked about.

> Just a reminder that the **bold** text in these lessons are suggestions for what you can say as you teach. Remember that this isn't a script; always feel free to take our ideas and put them in your own words.

Continue your discussion as a large group by asking questions like:

- **What connected the spies and Rahab?** *(They had to depend on each other. They all depended on God.)*
- **What differences did they overcome in order to connect?**
- **After reading this story, how do you think Rahab would define "fitting in"?** *(She chose to fit into God's plan.)*

- Why do you think this story with an immoral character is in the Bible? *(This is a good opportunity to remind students of the Key Verse: "Being confident of this, that he who began a good work in you will carry it to completion until the day of Christ Jesus" [Philippians 1:6].)*

In Joshua 6:17, we read that Rahab and her family were spared when Israel conquered the city. And to top that, she became an ancestor of Jesus! What an amazing way for a misfit to be connected.

Use these questions to prompt more large-group discussion:
- What were the key choices in this story?
- How could this story have turned out differently if Rahab and the spies refused to get connected to each other?
- What does this story tell us about the kind of people God accepts?

Rahab may have felt worthless—too far down the social ladder for God to care. But she turned to God anyway, and this social misfit became part of God's plan. The takeaway from today's story is this: Allow God in. He uses sinners who don't fit in to do what he wants done.

Take 3: Critics' Corner (15 to 20 minutes)

Setup: Reinforce the points you want your students to take away from today's lesson.
Props: Group journal with entries from Take 1; **Outtakes** (p. 62); beverage cups

QUIET ON THE SET
Grab the group journal and lead the group in reviewing their "2 Good 2 B 4-Gotten" entries recorded during Take 1.

ACTION
Consider the POV

Ask the group:
- Pick an answer: How quick are you to reject or judge others? a) sometimes; b) often; c) only if I have good reason; d) never. Why?

4: Earth Angel

Draw students' attention to the five answers from the Take 1 game written in the group journal, then ask:

- **As an outsider, how might Rahab have welcomed a friend's good laughs, good advice, good prayers, good gifts, and good times? What effect could they have had on her?**

Have everybody score the entries on the same "connect-ability" scale that they used in Take 1, but this time from Rahab's perspective; prompt them to consider how well each of the answers could make an outsider like Rahab feel connected to another person.

Discuss the idea that all sinners—including us—can find connection with God when we seek his grace. Then draw students' attention to the **POV** on the **Outtakes** handout: *We're not perfect—but God is approachable. Our commitment to him makes a difference.*

Lead your group in brainstorming small, unexpected ways they can help others feel connected to God's plan this week.

Understand God's Truth

God gets involved in imperfect lives. And he often does it in outside-the-box ways. Mistakes can't separate us from our heavenly Father when we commit our lives to him.

Ask the group:

- **What have you learned from today's story?** *(Don't judge a person by background or appearance. The spies might not have expected Rahab to turn to God, but she did.)*
- **What hope can we take away from Rahab's story?** *(God works in unexpected ways. Keep your heart and mind open).*
- **How does today's Key Verse illustrate the point of this story?**

God existed for Rahab the Not-So-Popular. His presence was real. She didn't live perfectly, but she asked for mercy and placed herself in his gracious hands.

Teamwork

Friendships matter! Remind your students of the powerful role they can play in encouraging each other's spiritual growth. Review some of the ideas students shared for ways they can help each other be connected to God, and encourage your group to put those ideas into action this week.

PLAY BACK

Wrap up the meeting with a let's-stay-connected team-building game and prayer.

Connect-the-Cup Stacks

Needed: foam or plastic beverage cups, masking or duct tape
Goal: Unstack and restack cups in relay fashion.

How to Play:

Use tape to create at least two lanes for play. In each lane, set up three cup-stacking stations with enough running room between each. At Station 1, make a three-cup pyramid by turning two cups over and stacking the third (open side down) on top, pyramid style. Station 2 will use six cups, three turned over, two on top (open side down), with the last cup stacked on top of that. Station 3 will use ten cups, four turned over, three cups followed by two, topped by the final cup.

Divide your group into two or more teams and have them form single-file lines at the start of each lane.

One player from each team should run to each cup station, unstack the cups, and then restack them just as they were. Once all three stations have been completed, the player should run back to his or her team and give the next person in line a high five; that next player can now begin. The winning team is the first to complete the relay.

For more challenging play, have students use just one hand to unstack and stack cups. Or have your students come up with their own stacking requirements. For example, cups can be stacked in a circular pattern (igloo-style) or in serpentine, domino-like lines.

Cup stacks topple when the connection is weak. The same is true of us: We need strong connections to get us through the tough times in life. A remarkable feature of life is that we *will* fail—spectacularly! So be God-dependent. Trust in him and stay connected to the right people.

4: Earth Angel

Close with Prayer

Ask your group to look again at **Outtakes** and repeat today's **Key Verse:** "Being confident of this, that he who began a good work in you will carry it on to completion until the day of Christ Jesus" (Philippians 1:6). Then point out *Verse-atility: God, finish the good work you started in me.* If time permits, jot the verse in the group journal and have everyone initial it.

Say: **This feature presentation had a twist ending: Not only did God come through for the spies, but he also met a sinner's needs.**

Take prayer requests, then lead the group in thanking God for the supernatural side of faith, its mystery and resiliency, and the role it plays in everyday life. ✘

Verse-atility: *God, finish the good work you started in me.*

Outtakes

CAST
Joshua: leader of the people of Israel
Spies: sent by Joshua to check out the land God promised to give Israel
Rahab: a prostitute living in a house on the wall around Jericho
King of Jericho: sends soldiers to find the spies
Soldiers: question Rahab and search for spies

MOVIE TRAILER
- Joshua sends two spies to check out Jericho. They go to Rahab's house.
- The king finds out the spies are there and sends soldiers to grab them.
- Rahab hides the spies and lies to the soldiers; the soldiers leave.
- Rahab tells the spies everyone knows how great their God is.
- Rahab asks the spies not to hurt her family in the battle. The spies agree.
- Rahab helps the spies escape safely over the city wall.

Verse-atility: God, finish the good work you started in me.

POV: We're not perfect—but God is approachable. Our commitment to him makes a difference.

Key Verse: Being confident of this, that he who began a good work in you will carry it on to completion until the day of Christ Jesus (Philippians 1:6).

EARTH ANGEL

Joshua 2:1-15 *(The Message)*
*(We've added a few of our own comments **in bold** below.)*

Joshua son of Nun secretly sent out from Shittim two men as spies:
  "Go. Look over the land. Check out Jericho." They left and arrived at the house of a harlot **[a.k.a. prostitute]** named Rahab and stayed there.
  The king of Jericho was told, "We've just learned that men arrived tonight to spy out the land. They're from the People of Israel."
  The king of Jericho sent word to Rahab: "Bring out the men who came to you to stay the night in your house. They're spies; they've come to spy out the whole country."
  The woman had taken the two men and hidden them. She said, "Yes, two men did come to me, but I didn't know where they'd come from. At dark, when the gate was about to be shut, the men left. But I have no idea where they went. Hurry up! Chase them—you can still catch them!" (She had actually taken them up on the roof and hidden them under the stalks of flax that were spread out for her on the roof.) **[A quick hideaway!]** So the men set chase down the Jordan road toward the fords. As soon as they were gone, the gate was shut.
  Before the spies were down for the night, the woman came up to them on the roof and said, "I know that God has given you the land. We're all afraid. Everyone in the country feels hopeless. We heard how God dried up the waters of the Red Sea before you when you left Egypt, and what he did to the two Amorite kings east of the Jordan, Sihon and Og, whom you put under a holy curse and destroyed. We heard it and our hearts sank. We all had the wind knocked out of us **[fatigue]**. And all because of you, you and God, your God, God of the heavens above and God of the earth below.
  "Now promise me by God. I showed you mercy; now show my family mercy. And give me some tangible proof, a guarantee of life for my father and mother, my brothers and sisters—everyone connected with my family. Save our souls from death!"
  "Our lives for yours!" said the men. "But don't tell anyone our business. When God turns this land over to us, we'll do right by you in loyal mercy" **[a deal maker]**.
  She lowered them down out a window with a rope because her house was on the city wall to the outside.

*Permission is granted by Standard Publishing to reproduce this **Outtakes** handout for ministry purposes only (not for resale).*

5 The Ghost Whisperer

Director's Commentary

NOW SHOWING: *The Ghost Whisperer*

FROM THE BIBLE: Saul consults the witch of Endor (1 Samuel 28:3-20).

RATED PG-13 FOR: witchcraft

POV: When God seems distant, think about how closely you're following him.

KEY VERSE: "My heart says of you, 'Seek his face!' Your face, Lord, I will seek" (Psalm 27:8).

The Lesson	Time	What you'll do . . .	How you'll do it . . .	What you'll need . . .
Take 1: Preview	15 to 20 minutes	Start off your lesson by introducing the theme with a relational, creative activity.	Option 1: Students act out "Action Hero" drama and discuss it.	Photocopies of "Action Hero" script (pp. 73, 74); markers, group journal supplies (*Optional:* items from your prop box, an Xbox 360 or other game system, nachos or popcorn, three sodas, jackets, movie snacks for your audience)
			Option 2: Students watch a DVD version of "Action Hero" and discuss it. Or, choose to do both.	*Shocking and Scandalous Stories from the Bible DVD*, TV and DVD player; group journal supplies
Take 2: Feature Presentation	15 to 20 minutes	Dive into the Bible story and explore it together.	Small group and large group discussion	Photocopies of **Outtakes** (p. 75); paper, clipboards, pens, large towels *Optional:* Bibles
Take 3: Critics' Corner	15 to 20 minutes	Help your students grasp God's point of view and wrap things up with a fun team-building activity	Discussion, game, and prayer	Photocopies of **Outtakes** (p. 75); group journal; 2 or more flashlights

Why Is This PG-13 Story in the Bible?

A fancy word is *necromancy*. It means trying to gain information by consulting with the dead. King Saul never should have gotten involved—he himself had banned it at a time when he was more in tune with God. But now he's anxious to know what's going to happen in an upcoming battle against Israel's nemesis: the Philistine army.

Saul has already tried asking God by consulting priests and prophets and hoping for a dream. But God is silent—he's withholding an answer from Saul because Saul's already well along on his downward spiral into a spiritual pit. God has already taken his Spirit from Saul and given it to David, the popular warrior and future king. Samuel, the prophet who anointed David and confronted Saul, is dead. Saul's so desperate that he gives the forbidden order for someone to find him a witch who can call up the spirit of Samuel.

That might sound spiritual, as if Saul genuinely wants the advice and reassurance of a man of God. But Saul's life by this time is one of unfaithfulness to God, and he's not especially sorry—just fearful of defeat in battle and perhaps his own death. He's looking for someone to tell him everything's going to be OK because he doesn't want to face the consequences of his own choices.

Does the witch really conjure up the spirit of Samuel? It's possible that this vision of Samuel was accomplished by satanic power. On the other hand, it's also possible that God permitted this to actually happen in order to get through to Saul. Either way, the witch shrieks when her efforts actually bring up Samuel—clearly this doesn't usually happen! She's used to pulling a few psychological tricks to figure out what people are thinking and telling them what they already know. But this time it's different. Samuel actually shows up with a message for Saul from God— and it's not the reassurance Saul is looking for. Samuel has no sympathy for the mess Saul has gotten himself into with his choices. He even predicts Saul's death in this battle, an event that comes true in 1 Samuel 31. God uses the witch to knock Saul in the head with the truth that God is the highest power and can do the unexpected.

Connecting with Community

Log on to www.shockingandscandalous.com to connect with other ministries:
- Check out a sample video of other students in action.
- Share with other leaders at the PG-13 forum about what's working in your ministry, what's not, or how you used *Shocking and Scandalous* this week.
- Or ask for input about other aspects of middle school ministry.

5: The Ghost Whisperer

This Bible story will help middle schoolers see that we can't treat God like a last-ditch resource when things go wrong. God wants relationship.

Take It to Your Students

Here are some key points to put in front of your students with this lesson:
- We can't manipulate God's power.
- Make God the first place you go, not the last.
- If God seems distant, examine how closely you're following him. ✗

The Ghost Whisperer: The Lesson

Take 1: Preview (15 to 20 minutes)

Setup: This activity will set up the day's Bible story in a relational way as students watch three friends weigh in on a parent's rule about sticking with age-appropriate video games.

Set design: Create a relaxed atmosphere for *Preview*. Ask students to sit on the floor in a circle on pillows, seat cushions, or colorful mats. The drama will be performed in the middle. Popcorn or movie snacks will help set a movie mood.

Makeup and effects: For today's drama, consider having students select props and costumes from your one-size-fits-all prop box.

Props: Supplies for the journal option you've chosen, markers; 4 copies of the "Action Hero" skit (pp. 73, 74) or the *Shocking and Scandalous Stories from the Bible DVD* and a TV with DVD player—or both
(*Optional:* items from your prop box, an Xbox 360 or other game system, nachos or chips, three sodas, jackets, movie snacks for you audience)

QUIET ON THE SET

To launch the lesson:
- Welcome everyone to the group. Use first names or preferred nicknames and introduce visitors. After your students have had some time to socialize, pull them in and have them get comfortable.

- Go over your Rules of Engagement, if needed. (See the Rules of Engagement suggestions on p. 6 for more information.)
- Review the journaling component you've chosen for your group. (See Create a Group Journal on p. 10 for more information.)

ACTION

Either have students perform the "Action Hero" skit, watch "Action Hero" on the *Shocking and Scandalous Stories from the Bible DVD*, or do both. If you choose to have students perform the skit live, give copies of the script to the actors and have them prep by reading through their parts a time or two. Also, invite the actors to rummage through the prop box for items to enhance the performance.

PLAY BACK

Spend some time talking about "Action Hero" with your group; use the questions below to guide your group's discussion. Don't edit students' responses—allow them to discuss freely. Have a volunteer jot "Action Hero" and today's date in the group journal and record the group's impressions. As usual, allow everyone time to comment or to journal, even if it's just to initial in agreement with posted entries.

John has great gaming skills. And now something's come up—an opportunity, as he sees it, to have fun without technically having to break the house rules.

Use these questions to get the discussion going:
- What does Lucas want John to do? Why?
- Should being faithful to his mother's wishes be an important consideration for John? If so, how big a factor should it be? Explain.
- Have you ever been in a situation like this—when your parents' rules are much more strict than what your friends get to see, play with, or participate in? Give an example.
- Evaluate John's decision. Did he do the right thing in your eyes? Is it really such a big deal? Explain your thoughts.
- How does John's decision reflect what's most important to him?

You're growing up and you want to make your own decisions. But no matter what our age, we all answer to a higher authority.

5: The Ghost Whisperer

Up next: We'll meet an absolutely freaked-out ruler, who sets out on an illegal witch hunt for clues to his own mortality. Terror and the realm-of-the-dead co-star in today's PG-13 filmmaker's adaptation, *The Ghost Whisperer*. ✘

Take 2: Feature Presentation (15 to 20 minutes)

Setup: Your students will take a close look at the story of Saul and the witch of Endor and discuss walking closely with God.
Props: Photocopies of **Outtakes** (p. 75); paper, clipboards, pens, large towels
   Optional: Bibles

QUIET ON THE SET

Pass out copies of **Outtakes**, one per student. *Optional:* Have students grab their Bibles.

ACTION

Use **Outtakes** to introduce and teach the Bible story. First, briefly introduce the **Cast** and make sure your students know who's who. Next, use **Movie Trailer** to cover the highlights of the Bible background and story. Then read the Bible story (1 Samuel 28:3-20) out loud from **Outtakes** or have a volunteer read it. If you prefer, ask students to read the passage aloud from their own Bibles.

PLAY BACK

Divide your group into two or more small teams for discussion with an adult or older teen leader for each group. Have about half of the groups talk about the witch of Endor (Team Talk 1) and the remaining groups look into Saul's point of view (Team Talk 2). Remind group leaders to be ready to enhance discussion with insights from **Why Is This PG-13 Story in the Bible?** (p. 64).

> Just a reminder that we've got some helpful insights about forming small groups in the Team Talk Small Groups section on pp. 10, 11.

Give each small group a clipboard with paper on it, a pen, and a large towel. Have students discuss and write about the motivations they see in the story characters. To do so, have them drape the towel (representing a prophet's robe) over one student to start. Anyone may talk during the discussion, but the student with the robe and clipboard will write a few answers or impressions during the discussion. At random intervals, the group leader can take the towel and drape it on another student as a signal to pass the clipboard while continuing discussion.

Let's get inside the heads of Saul and the witch.

Team Talk 1: Get in the head of the witch.

- **The witch knows that what she does has been outlawed. Why do you suppose she's still in business?** *(Because people still come to her for the service she provides. She can make money.)*
- **The witch seems cautious. Why would this be?** *(She's afraid of the consequences if she's caught.)*
- **What do you think might have motivated her to say yes to this stranger's request?** *(She wants to make money. The stranger promises she won't get in trouble.)*
- **What do you think the woman felt or thought when Samuel appears?** *(She's surprised. Usually what she does is just tricks. This time something really happens. She sees God's power at work!)*

Team Talk 2: Get in the head of Saul.

- **What is it that Saul's after? Is he seeking God, or is it something else he wants? Explain your point of view.** *(He's seeking God for the wrong reason—just to get good news, not for a real relationship.)*
- **Why is Saul desperate enough to consult a witch?** *(God is silent. God is not speaking to him by any other method.)*
- **Exposed! Saul wears a disguise. What does this show is going on in his heart?** *(He knows consulting a medium is wrong and doesn't want anyone to know it is him.)*
- **How do you suppose Saul feels when he hears what the spirit of Samuel has to say?** *(It's not what he was hoping to hear; now he has anxiety-overload. He is seriously freaked out!)*

Bring the discussion groups back together. Briefly review results of discussions by talking through some of the notes written on the clipboards and inviting students to elaborate.

Continue your discussion as a large group by asking questions like:
- **So, does this story mean it's OK to try to conjure up ghosts? Why or why not?** *(No. The story is in the Bible to show God's power.)*

- How would you describe what's in Saul's heart based on this story? *(Conflict, conflict, conflict.)*
- Saul was facing some serious anxiety. When you're stressed about the unknown, what do you usually do? What helps you get through it?
- How does having Scripture in your heart help in anxious times? When have you experienced this? *(Point out today's Key Verse: "My heart says of you, 'Seek his face!' Your face, Lord, I will seek" [Psalm 27:8].)*

Virtual God? Saul knows his relationship with God is fuzzy. He hasn't been truly following him for a long time. But now he's desperate to shake off his fear and get some positive indicators about an upcoming battle and his kingship. He treats God like a last-ditch effort when things go wrong, rather than staying close to God all the time.

Use these questions to prompt more large-group discussion:
- What choices might have changed this story?
- How is Saul's story an example of looking for answers in all the wrong places?
- What's one life lesson you can learn from Saul's story?

A dark spirit haunts Saul. And it isn't otherworldly. It's fear.

Like he did with Saul, God wants a relationship with you. He's not looking to be a magician for desperate moments like Saul wanted him to be. So when God seems distant, think about how closely you're following him. ✘

Take 3: Critics' Corner (15 to 20 minutes)

Setup: Reinforce the points you want your students to take away from today's lesson.
Props: Group journal with entries from Take 1; **Outtakes** (p. 75); 2 or more flashlights

QUIET ON THE SET

Grab the group journal and ask students to gather to review the "Action Hero" entries recorded during Take 1.

ACTION

Consider the POV

Review the entries from the opening "Action Hero" skit from the group journal.

Ask:

- Can John's mother count on him? Why or why not?
- John's mom would be disappointed with his decision. How might this affect their relationship? *(Strained, suspicious, hurt)*
- Who shares responsibility for John's decision? *(No one! John is responsible for his decision.)*
- What can John do to avoid a repeat of the problem? *(Reliability is job number one; honor his mother's rules: demonstrate respect and consideration. Learn to say no.)*
- How do you think God feels when we're unfaithful to him? *(Hurt, betrayed)*

Use today's **POV** (*When God seems distant, think about how closely you're following him*) to lead your group in discussing and deciding on a new and improved ending for the skit. (If you want, have the actors perform the new ending for the group.)

Understand God's Truth

When Saul doesn't hear from God, he ditches him, desperate to try something else. Saul's unfaithfulness has severe consequences: God removes his Spirit from Saul.

Ask the group:

- What have we learned from today's story? *(Saul acted in desperation because he wasn't hearing from God, so instead he turned to something he knew was wrong.)*
- Name two "must-haves" for any positive relationship, whether with another person or with God. *(Faithfulness and respect.)*

Today, God gives his Holy Spirit to all of who believe in Jesus and have a relationship with him. Though we might ignore the Spirit at times, God doesn't take him away from us. But as the ultimate power source, God refuses to be treated like a last-ditch resource. A true relationship requires faithfulness—it's high on God's requirement list. When we treat it lightly as Saul did, we disrespect the sacredness of that relationship.

5: The Ghost Whisperer

Teamwork

Keep your eye on God! Be young men and women of faithfulness this week, committed to your creator and to each other.

PLAY BACK

Wrap up the meeting with a team-building game that tests players' faithfulness and perseverance. Then close in prayer.

Night at the Museum

Needed: 2 or more flashlights
Goal: Don't get caught moving!

> If you've got a large group, have players who are caught moving act as additional night watchmen with flashlights. If your group is small, have anyone caught moving replace the watchman.

How to Play:

"Hire" two night watchmen and give them flashlights. Have them face the wall or wait outside for further instructions. (If your group is small, use only one watchman.)

Tell the rest of your group they will spend a night at the museum. Ask them to spread throughout the "museum" (the room) and freeze in place like statues on display. Turn out the lights or darken the room the best you can. Invite your watchmen back into the room. Ask them to turn on their flashlights and start walking through the museum looking for any "unauthorized movement."

Any time during play, "statues" may change position or location just as long as the watchmen don't catch them doing it! Watchmen cannot touch statues, but they can try and make them laugh or move with silly comments like "Statue, statue, I saw you move! Statue, statue, get down and groove!"

If a statue responds or moves, he or she sits out play. The statue that remains faithful to his or her performance the longest wins.

> **Verse-atility:** *Lord, I will keep both eyes on you!*

God desires a faithful relationship with you—a relationship that will stand strong, no matter what. The all-powerful, all-wonderful creator wants to walk beside you twenty-four-seven and share your heart. He's not distant. His Spirit is near. Talk to him.

Close with Prayer

Ask your group to look again at **Outtakes** and repeat today's **Key Verse:** "My heart says of you, 'Seek his face!' Your face, Lord, I will seek" (Psalm 27:8). Then point out *Verse-atility,* a friendly rewording of today's Key Verse: *Lord, I will keep both eyes on you!* Encourage your students to keep God's truth front and center in their lives this week. If time permits, jot the verse in the group journal and have everyone initial it.

Listen for prayer requests and lead the group in praying for them. Also pray that God would help your students live out a faithful, consistent relationship with God. ✘

Action Hero

Characters: JOHN, PATRICK, and LUCAS: three middle school boys; CARLA: John's sister (either an older teen or college-aged)

Scene: JOHN'S house—family room or bedroom. The boys are sitting on a couch, bed, or beanbags playing video games and eating popcorn or nachos and drinking pop.

Prop Suggestions: Select any props or costumes you want from the prop box. Also, if you want, use a TV, video game controllers, and Xbox 360 or other gaming system (or just pretend!).

SCRIPT

(As it opens, LUCAS and PATRICK are playing video games while JOHN watches. The boys make little eye contact—they're mostly looking toward the TV.)

PATRICK:
(playing intently, but also eyeing John's popcorn) **Hey, gimme some.**

JOHN:
(speaking with light sarcasm to his friend) **You should say "please" or "may I" when you want something.**

PATRICK:
OK, may I *please* have some? Or I *may* beat you!

JOHN:
Very funny.

(Both laugh. John shoves the popcorn over.)

LUCAS:
(playing, but bored) **When are we gonna play something good or something cool? This game is for, like, six-year-olds.**

JOHN:
My mom told me I'm only allowed to play E10 and up in ESRBs for now.

PATRICK:
ESP? **What's that?**

JOHN:
E-S-R-B. The Entertainment Software Rating Board. . . . *(Patrick interrupts John . . .)*

PATRICK:
Why do you even *know* that? *(John laughs a little and continues with his first answer . . .)*

JOHN:
. . . It gives info to parents on video games—violence, bad language, blood and gore. Stuff like that.

PATRICK:
(with mouth full of food and a look of disbelief) **What??**

LUCAS:
(pointing to the box; somewhat of a mocking look on his face because he thinks the rule is dumb) **The little symbols on the front of the box. The rating system.**

PATRICK:
(shaking his head in recognition) **Oh, yeah. That.**

JOHN:
It hasn't really been that big of a deal.

LUCAS:
My brother says the best games are rated M.

JOHN:
M for mature? Yeah right. I'd never be allowed to play those.

LUCAS:
Then let's go to my house. My brother's not home. He won't even know I touched his games.

PATRICK:
(wiping his hands on his pants, mouth full of food) **You got any food at your house?**

(John's not quite sure how to react to this sudden change in plans.)

LUCAS:
C'mon, man. Your mom's out of town—she won't even know. Parents take this stuff way too seriously. It's just a video game.

JOHN:
(thinking to himself—talking to the guys but thinking it through out loud) **Yeah, I guess you're right. It's only a game. As long as I'm not breaking house rules, I don't see what the problem is. It's not like we're gonna bring the game back here . . .**

(John's older sister Carla enters the room. . . .)

JOHN:
(starts to get up to get his coat) **OK . . . I'm in . . . but I go first!**

CARLA:
Where are you going?

PATRICK:
(quietly, and tapping Lucas) **Uh-oh.**

CARLA:
We told Mom and Dad we'd get the whole garage cleaned out, remember?

JOHN:
(Looking somewhat guilty) **Uh. I'll get Lucas's mom to give me a ride back here.**

CARLA:
(Looking very doubtfully at her younger brother) **John, I'm *really* counting on your help tonight. OK?**

JOHN:
(feeling a bit of guilt) **Don't worry. You can count on me . . . See ya.**

(Carla turns and walks out of the room. She isn't very sure her brother is going to come through . . .)

JOHN:
Guys—let's go.

Permission is granted by Standard Publishing to reproduce this "Action Hero" script for ministry purposes only (not for resale).

Outtakes

CAST

Samuel: God's prophet to Israel; he has died
Saul: the king of Israel, who has turned away from God
Witch: the woman Saul asks to help him speak to the dead prophet

MOVIE TRAILER

- The Philistines, the arch-enemies of God's people, are getting ready to battle Israel.
- Saul wants God's assurance that everything is going to be OK, but God doesn't speak to him because of his disobedient ways.
- Even though he knows better, Saul hopes a witch can help him.
- Saul disguises himself and consults the witch, but she discovers who he really is.
- Samuel's spirit appears to tell Saul that he will die in the battle.

Verse-atility: Lord, I will keep both eyes on you!

POV: When God seems distant, think about how closely you're following him.

Key Verse: My heart says of you, "Seek his face!" Your face, Lord, I will seek (Psalm 27:8).

THE GHOST WHISPERER

1 Samuel 28:3-20 *(The Message)*
*(We've added a few of our own comments **in bold** below.)*

Samuel was now dead. All Israel had mourned his death and buried him in Ramah, his hometown. Saul had long since cleaned out all those who held séances with the dead.

The Philistines had mustered their troops and camped at Shunem. Saul had assembled all Israel and camped at Gilboa. But when Saul saw the Philistine troops, he shook in his boots, scared to death.

Saul prayed to God, but God didn't answer—neither by dream nor by sign nor by prophet.

So Saul ordered his officials, "Find me someone who can call up spirits **[he's looking for good luck charms?]** so I may go and seek counsel from those spirits."

His servants said, "There's a witch at Endor."

Saul disguised himself by putting on different clothes. Then, taking two men with him, he went under the cover of night to the woman and said, "I want you to consult a ghost for me. **[Virtual reality!]** Call up the person I name."

The woman said, "Just hold on now! You know what Saul did, how he swept the country clean of mediums. Why are you trying to trap me and get me killed?"

Saul swore solemnly, "As God lives, you won't get in any trouble for this."

The woman said, "So whom do you want me to bring up?"

"Samuel. Bring me Samuel."

When the woman saw Samuel, she cried out loudly to Saul, "Why did you lie to me? You're Saul!"

The king told her, "You have nothing to fear . . . but what do you see?"

"I see a spirit ascending from the underground."

"And what does he look like?" Saul asked.

"An old man ascending, robed like a priest."

Saul knew it was Samuel. He fell down, face to the ground, and worshiped.

Samuel said to Saul, "Why have you disturbed me by calling me up?" **[Samuel on the rise—*creepy* . . .]**

"Because I'm in deep trouble," said Saul. "The Philistines are making war against me and God has deserted me—he doesn't answer me any more, either by prophet or by dream. And so I'm calling on you to tell me what to do."

"Why ask me?" said Samuel. "God has turned away from you **[warning sign!]** and is now on the side of your neighbor. God has done exactly what he told you through me—ripped the kingdom right out of your hands and given it to your neighbor. It's because you did not obey God, refused to carry out his seething judgment on Amalek, that God does to you what he is doing today. Worse yet, God is turning Israel, along with you, over to the Philistines. Tomorrow you and your sons will be with me. And, yes, indeed, God is giving Israel's army up to the Philistines."

Saul dropped to the ground, felled like a tree, terrified by Samuel's words.

Permission is granted by Standard Publishing to reproduce this **Outtakes** handout for ministry purposes only (not for resale).

6 Risky Business

Director's Commentary

NOW SHOWING: *Risky Business*
FROM THE BIBLE: David and Bathsheba (2 Samuel 11:2-5, 8-11, 14-17, 26, 27; 12:1-7).
RATED PG-13 FOR: voyeurism, sexual content, and murder
POV: Put one foot in front of the other and run from tempting situations. Trying to cover up sin only makes things worse.
KEY VERSE: "Have mercy on me, O God, according to your unfailing love; according to your great compassion blot out my transgressions" (Psalm 51:1).

The Lesson	Time	What you'll do . . .	How you'll do it . . .	What you'll need . . .
Take 1: Preview	15 to 20 minutes	Start off your lesson by introducing the theme with a relational, creative activity.	Option 1: Students act out "Secret Shopper" drama and discuss it.	Photocopies of "Secret Shopper" script (pp. 86, 87); markers, group journal supplies (*Optional*: items from your prop box; a digital camera, two-way radio or walkie-talkie, purse, pair of earrings, shopping bag, movie snacks for your audience)
			Option 2: Students watch a DVD version of "Secret Shopper" and discuss it. Or, choose to do both.	*Shocking and Scandalous Stories from the Bible* DVD, TV and DVD player; group journal supplies
Take 2: Feature Presentation	15 to 20 minutes	Dive into the Bible story and explore it together.	Small group and large group discussion	Photocopies of **Outtakes** (pp. 88, 89); sheets of newsprint, markers *Optional*: Bibles
Take 3: Critics' Corner	15 to 20 minutes	Help your students grasp God's point of view and wrap things up with a fun team-building activity.	Discussion, game, and prayer	Photocopies of **Outtakes** (pp. 88, 89); group journal; 2 or more plastic junior bat and ball sets, masking tape, marker

6: Risky Business

Why Is This PG-13 Story in the Bible?

No one says no to the king! David knows this and is prepared to use his power for personal advantage. On a warm night, David wanders out to the flat roof of his palace looking for cool air. Height gives him a vantage point that reveals a beautiful woman on a rooftop taking a bath. He wants her, plain and simple. David dispatches someone to fetch her. The messengers know she is a married woman whose husband is away, but they don't say no to the king.

Bathsheba arrives. In a culture in which women are barely above the status of property, it's possible she has little choice in the matter. Add to that the fact that the one issuing the summons is the powerful king, and it's easy to imagine that Bathsheba feels she has no option but to go to his bed. She doesn't say no to the king.

A few weeks later she discovers she's pregnant. The law would have prescribed death for both David and Bathsheba, but who's going to kill the popular king? David has nothing to fear from the law. Nevertheless, he goes to a great deal of trouble to cover up his sin. Most likely, he's trying to protect his own honor and Bathsheba's as well. He's concerned about appearance and reputation—he has an image to protect.

David never should have done what he did, but attempting to cover it up just makes the mess bigger. Springtime is battle season. David summons Bathsheba's husband Uriah home under the guise of asking for a report on the war. The real reason? David wants Uriah to sleep with his wife Bathsheba so that he will think the baby is his. But things don't turn out like David wants. Uriah gives a report, but he doesn't go home to his wife—not even for one night. How can he think about sex when the ark of the Lord (the chest that represents the presence of God) is at the battlefront? David is determined to cover up his sin, so he purposely has Uriah assigned to the front line—where he is killed. This leaves Bathsheba free to marry David.

The prophet Nathan confronts David, and David finally acknowledges his sin. God reminds David—and us—that his law is higher than the king's

> **Connecting with Community**
> Log on to www.shockingandscandalous.com to connect with other ministries:
> - Check out a sample video of other students in action.
> - Share with other leaders at the PG-13 forum about what's working in your ministry, what's not, or how you used *Shocking and Scandalous* this week.
> - Or ask for input about other aspects of middle school ministry.

power. This Bible story will help middle schoolers see that once sin gets started, it's hard to stop.

Take It to Your Students

Here are some key points to put in front of your students with this lesson:
- The best thing to do in a tempting situation is to run the other way.
- Trying to cover up sin only makes it worse.
- Even small decisions can lead to painful consequences. ✗

Risky Business: The Lesson

Take 1: Preview (15 to 20 minutes)

Setup: This activity will set up the day's Bible story in a relational way as students listen to the "Secret Shopper" tale of regret.

Set design: Create a relaxed atmosphere for *Preview*. Ask students to sit on the floor in a circle on pillows, seat cushions, or colorful mats. The drama will be performed in the middle. Popcorn or movie snacks will help set a movie mood.

Props: The journal option you've chosen, markers; 1 photocopy of the "Secret Shopper" skit (pp. 86, 87)

(*Optional:* items from your prop box, a digital camera, two-way radio or walkie-talkie, purse, pair of earrings, shopping bag, movie snacks for your audience)

QUIET ON THE SET
- Welcome everyone to the group. Use first names or preferred nicknames and introduce visitors. After your students have had some time to socialize, pull them in and have them get comfortable.
- Go over your Rules of Engagement, if needed. (See the Rules of Engagement suggestions on p. 6 for more information.)
- Review the journaling component you've chosen for your group. (See Create a Group Journal on p. 10 for more information.)

ACTION

Either have students perform the "Secret Shopper" skit, watch "Secret Shopper" on the *Shocking and Scandalous Stories from the Bible DVD*, or do both. If you choose to have students perform the skit live, give a copy of the script to a female student who will play the lead role and have her prep by reading through the script a few times. Also select one or two other students to have nonspeaking roles as mall security guards. Invite the actors to rummage through the prop box and select items to use or wear; if you have them, give actors the camera, a two-way radio (this is the only prop for the guards, by the way!), a purse, a pair of earrings, and a shopping bag.

Option: If you want, make a video of your students' live performance. Play it back later (perhaps for the entire church).

PLAY BACK

Reflect on "Secret Shopper" with your group using the discussion suggestions below. Don't edit your students' responses—allow them to speak freely. As everyone talks together, have a volunteer record the group's impressions and feelings about "Secret Shopper" in the group journal. Jot "Secret Shopper" and today's date at the top of the journal entry. Give every student the opportunity to comment or to journal, even if it's just to initial in agreement with posted entries.

We heard a very personal experience in today's skit. Let's talk more about "Secret Shopper."

Use these questions to get the discussion going:

- How did the skit make you feel? Why?
- Is temptation real for Secret Shopper? How did she handle it?
- Do you think Secret Shopper knew what she would do before entering the store? Why or why not?
- Acting above the law led to the mess Secret Shopper is in. How did her desire lead to regret?
- What is Secret Shopper's impression of herself? Of the cheerleading squad? Of her parents?
- How do *you* handle tempting situations? Very well, kind of average, or not so good? Explain.

SHOCKING AND SCANDALOUS STORIES FROM THE BIBLE

If only we could rewind our mistakes and start new. Today's presentation shines the spotlight on a pivotal character, a one-man show. This star's desire for another man's wife shatters his popular image—along with a few of God's commandments. Desire and calculated murder in *Risky Business*, up next. ✘

Take 2: Feature Presentation (15 to 20 minutes)

Setup: Your students will take a close look at the story of David and Bathsheba and discuss handling temptation.

Props: Photocopies of **Outtakes** (pp. 88, 89), large sheets of newsprint, and markers
   Optional: Bibles

QUIET ON THE SET

Pass out copies of **Outtakes**, one per student.
Optional: Have students grab their Bibles.

ACTION

Use **Outtakes** to introduce and teach the Bible story. First, briefly introduce the **Cast** and make sure your students know who's who. Next, use **Movie Trailer** to cover the highlights of the Bible background and story. Then read the Bible story (2 Samuel 11:2-5, 8-11, 14-17, 26, 27; 12:1-7) out loud from **Outtakes** or have volunteers read it. If you prefer, ask students to read the passages aloud from their own Bibles.

PLAY BACK

Divide your group into two or more small teams for discussion with an adult or older teen leader for each group. If possible, plan to make the groups all guys or all girls. Guys will look into the lives of David, Uriah, and Nathan (Guy Talk); girls will explore things from Bathsheba's point of view (Girl Talk). If your group is small, you can discuss all the questions together, but choose discussion questions with sensitivity. Remind group leaders to be ready to enhance discussion with insights from **Why Is This PG-13 Story in the Bible?** (p. 77).

Give each small group a large sheet of newsprint and markers. Have the girls write "Bathsheba" at the top of their sheet. Have the guys mark off three sections, one each for "David," "Uriah," and "Nathan." Direct the groups to discuss and write about the motivations they see in the story characters by making a list of as many words as they can think of that describe each character.

This story is full of turning points and choices with consequences. Let's get into the characters' heads and do a little exploring.

Guy Talk: Get into the heads of David, Uriah, and Nathan.

- In your opinion, what was the main motivation for David's actions in this story? *(Getting what he wanted, including sex; protecting his image.)*
- How did David drag others into his sin? *(He made messengers get Bathsheba; he seduced Bathsheba; he used his general, Joab, to murder Uriah.)*
- Uriah could have slept with his wife when he was on leave from the battle. How does his attitude about sex contrast with David's? *(David indulged his desires instead of doing the right thing; Uriah kept his focus on doing the right thing as a soldier rather than giving in to temptation.)*
- What was Nathan's job in this story? *(To correct David; to make David repent.)*
- How do you think Nathan felt about doing this job? Would *you* want that job? Why or why not?

Girl Talk: Get into the head of Bathsheba.

- In what ways was Bathsheba caught in the middle of things? *(She perhaps could not say no to the king, yet she cheated on her husband.)*
- How would you imagine Bathsheba felt when the king wanted her? Could that have affected her choices? *(She might have liked feeling wanted and allowed his attention.)*
- Bathsheba is often thought of as a temptress, and she often gets a lot of the blame for what happened between her and David. What do *you* think? Is she at fault—or is she a victim? Defend your answer.
- Do women in movies today often act like Bathsheba in the parts they play? Explain.
- Would Jesus buy a ticket to see such a flick? Why or why not? Explain.

Bring the groups back together. Briefly review results of discussions by inviting volunteers to highlight the key words they listed on their sheets of newsprint.

Continue your discussion as a large group by asking questions like:
- **What consequences did the choices in this story lead to?** *(Emotional pain; unwanted pregnancy; involving innocent people—messengers, Joab—in sin; death of an innocent man)*
- **What was the point of Nathan's story?** *(To make David realize he could not cover up his sin.)*
- **Why do you think this story about adultery and murder is in the Bible?**

Fact pattern. David wanted what he wanted. It was an easy slide into temptation. Nathan reminded David that he was not above God's law and would need to face his sin. Later, Bathsheba's baby died. So many people were hurt by a decision made in a passionate moment.

Use these questions to kick off more large-group discussion:
- **Could things have turned out differently? Identify the places where a different choice could have changed the outcome of this story.**
- **What do we learn from this story about handling tempting situations?** *(Run the other direction!)*
- **How does the Key Verse (Psalm 51:1) reflect the attitude we should have when we sin? Explain it in your own words.** *(Repentance; depend on God for forgiveness)*

> If your students are interested, invite volunteers to read Psalm 51 aloud for the group. Or, if you're short on time, challenge your students to read Psalm 51 on their own during the week.

Nathan's wisdom hits home. When he comes face to face with his sin, David writes Psalm 51, the source of today's Bible verse. In it he expresses how sorry he is for his choices. Learn from David's mistakes. Put one foot in front of the other and run from tempting situations. As we've seen, trying to cover up sin only makes things worse. ✗

Take 3: Critics' Corner (15 to 20 minutes)

Setup: Reinforce the points you want your students to take away from today's lesson.

6: Risky Business

Props: Group journal with entries from Take 1; **Outtakes** (pp. 88, 89); 2 or more plastic junior bat and ball sets, masking tape, marker

QUIET ON THE SET

Grab the group journal and ask students to gather to review their initial thoughts and impressions from "Secret Shopper" recorded during Take 1.

ACTION

Consider the POV

Discuss the role temptation plays in your students' lives. Ask the group:

- What would have been the better choice for Secret Shopper? Why?
- Think about temptation and covering things up. Do you sometimes allow others to make decisions for you so you don't have to take responsibility for your actions? Have you ever tried to cover things up? Share from your own experiences.
- Giving in to temptation can cause some major inner turmoil! How does giving in to temptation affect a person? What struggles does it bring? *(It's hard to keep secrets we know are wrong; it's hard to live two lives.)*
- True or False: Fleeing from temptation is hard. *(True!)*

> If you think the students in your group will be hesitant to share some of their own struggles with temptation in front of the whole group, mix things up by having students form pairs to talk through these discussion questions. It's a lot easier to open up one-on-one.

Record students' insights in the group journal, then draw their attention to the **POV** on the **Outtakes** handout: *Put one foot in front of the other and run from tempting situations. Trying to cover up sin only makes things worse.*

Understand God's Truth

Once you give in to temptation, it's pretty hard to stop. Like ripples in a pond, small decisions lead to mistakes and final consequences. We are reminded by God's Word to run from tempting times.

Ask the group:

- What have we learned from today's story? *(David gave in to temptation and spent a lot of effort trying to cover things up. Covering up doesn't make the sin go away.)*

- **What helps with good decision making?** *(Keep God's Word. Don't ignore your "early warning system"—the little voice inside that tells you something's wrong.)*

Like David, popularity doesn't grant us special privileges to do whatever we want. Having an image to protect doesn't mean we're above God's laws. His standards are higher than our own.

Teamwork

It takes courage to do the right thing—more so when no one is looking. Don't back down! Join the resistance! Let's support each other throughout the week to keep temptation from wrecking our good choices.

PLAY BACK

Wrap up the meeting with a team-building activity that helps students think about battling temptation. Then close in prayer.

Temptation Battle

Needed: 2 or more plastic junior bat and ball sets, masking tape, marker
Goal: Keep a "temptation" ball out of their team's area.

How to Play:

First, use masking tape to mark two parallel lines on the floor, about 15 feet apart. (Use spray paint for outdoor play.) Write the word "temptation" on a small piece of tape and attach it to a plastic ball.

Divide your group into two equal teams (rotate in extra players, if necessary). Have teams line up behind their assigned line and face each other. Ask each team to count off so that every student is assigned a number. (You'll have two "1s," two "2s," two "3s," and so on.)

> Rather than purchasing plastic bats and balls, you can use sturdy wooden spoons in place of bats and tennis balls instead of the plastic ones.

Begin play by shouting out a number. The two players with that number will meet in the center. Hand each a plastic bat. Drop the "temptation" ball into play. The two players will now battle it out to try and tap, nudge, swipe, and hit the ball across the line of the opposing team. Teams must try and stop "temptation" from entering their zone with hands or feet or any other way they can without crossing their line. (With large groups and with extra supplies, you can call out two, three, or more numbers at a time and watch players battle temptation in force!)

One last thing: Today's media glamorizes physical intimacy between unmarried couples as a good thing without any risks. We now know better, don't we? Hollywood and the entertainment industry are not concerned with the real world or real relationships. Its products are fiction—make-believe. God's standards are for the real world *you* live in.

Close with Prayer

Ask your group to look again at **Outtakes** and repeat today's **Key Verse:** "Have mercy on me, O God, according to your unfailing love; according to your great compassion blot out my transgressions" (Psalm 51:1). Then point out this week's *Verse-atility*, a personalized re-wording of the Key Verse: *Loving God, wipe away my wrongs*. If time permits, jot the verse in the group journal and have everyone initial it.

Together, brainstorm some ways teens and preteens can portray a positive and wholesome image with God's help. Invite them to share prayer requests, then pray for them. Conclude by praying about your students' efforts to resist temptation with God's help. ✘

Verse-atility: *Loving God, wipe away my wrongs.*

Secret Shopper

Characters: SECRET SHOPPER, a teen girl; Optional: one or two mall security guards (nonspeaking roles)
Scene: A holding room in a mall's security area
Prop Suggestions: Select any props or costumes you want from the prop box. Also, if you want, use a handheld camera or phone that takes video, two-way radio (for the guard), purse, pair of earrings still in their packaging, and shopping bag (or just pretend).

SCRIPT

(Throughout, SECRET SHOPPER talks directly into her handheld camera or phone, occasionally looking away or down, but always holding her camera or phone out in front of her.)

SECRET SHOPPER:
(Speaking emotionally, worn-out, sad—occasionally voice cracks with emotion, occasionally close to tears as talking.)

This is the first time I ever broke the law. It's like a nightmare. . . . I can't believe this is happening to me. I know it was a mistake . . . one bad choice in one split second. . . . I just wish I'd done the right thing.

It was just a normal day at the mall. Steph and I were shopping around, and we decided to go get some jewelry and stuff at a store on the upper level. I wanted some new earrings, so I walked around the store looking. I found a pair I thought I might want.

(Optional: hold up earrings, still in their packaging)

So I went to show them to Steph. She was in the front of the store. It was obvious she was bored and ready to go.

So . . . we just walked out.

It wasn't until we were about halfway through the mall that I realized I still had the earrings in my hand. I suddenly felt sick inside. I'd *stolen* them.

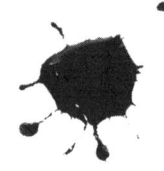

I knew I *could* take the earrings back and tell the clerk it was a mistake and hope she didn't call security . . . or . . . I could just walk back in and leave them on the rack . . . assuming that she hadn't already called security. . . . Or I could just ignore the whole thing and hope I wasn't caught.

(Girl looks at the camera for a few seconds in silence and then sighs.)

Who am I kidding?

The truth is I thought I could get away with it. And, you know what? . . .

(looks down at the table and than back at the camera, embarrassed)

. . . once you start, it's really hard to stop.

So . . . I just kept walking. But soon the security guard caught up with us.

(Optional: Secret Shopper refers to the security guard behind her with her eyes, or a gesture)

He made Steph and me wait at the escalators for the clerk to come identify me. I told him that I didn't need to steal; I had money. But he'd heard that line before. He looked at me just like all the other shoplifters he'd ever caught.

That *hurt*.

When the clerk got there, she took one quick look and nodded her head. "Yeah, that's her." When she said that—when she looked at me like that—I just wanted to die. It was the worst, the lowest, I've ever felt.

So here I am, waiting for my parents to pick me up. The store is pressing charges and I have to go to court. Steph says I'll probably get kicked off the cheerleading squad.

I know I messed up. I *really* messed up. I was tempted and I gave in.

I just hope my parents can forgive me.

I hope *God* can forgive me. I mean, if he can forgive me, then maybe I can forgive myself.

(Secret Shopper shuts her phone or turns off her camera; video ends.)

(Actors rejoin group.)

Permission is granted by Standard Publishing to reproduce this "Secret Shopper" script for ministry purposes only (not for resale).

Outtakes

CAST
David: king of Israel and Judah
Bathsheba: wife of Uriah, living near the palace
Uriah: a soldier fighting at the front lines
Joab: David's general
Nathan: God's prophet

MOVIE TRAILER
- From his rooftop, the popular and powerful King David sees Bathsheba bathing.
- David seduces Bathsheba, and they have sex.
- Bathsheba discovers she's pregnant, and David decides to cover up their sin.
- David brings Uriah home hoping he will sleep with Bathsheba and everyone will think the baby is his.
- Uriah doesn't sleep with his wife, so David arranges with Joab for Uriah to be killed in battle.
- The prophet Nathan confronts David with the horror of what he has done.

POV: Put one foot in front of the other and run from tempting situations. Trying to cover up sin only makes things worse.

Key Verse: Have mercy on me, O God, according to your unfailing love; according to your great compassion blot out my transgressions (Psalm 51:1).

RISKY BUSINESS
2 Samuel 11:2-5, 8-11, 14-17, 26, 27; 12:1-7 *(The Message)*
*(We've added a few of our own comments **in bold** below.)*

One late afternoon, David got up from taking his nap and was strolling on the roof of the palace. From his vantage point on the roof he saw a woman bathing. The woman was stunningly beautiful. David sent to ask about her, and was told, "Isn't this Bathsheba, daughter of Eliam and wife of Uriah the Hittite?" David sent his agents to get her. After she arrived, he went to bed with her. **[Parental advisory sticker!]** . . . Then she returned home. Before long she realized she was pregnant. Later she sent word to David: "I'm pregnant."

[So David thought up a plan and called Bathsheba's husband Uriah home from the battlefield.]

. . . Then he said to Uriah, "Go home. Have a refreshing bath and a good night's rest."

After Uriah left the palace, an informant of the king was sent after him. But Uriah didn't go home. He slept that night at the palace entrance, along with the king's servants.

David was told that Uriah had not gone home. He asked Uriah, "Didn't you just come off a hard trip? So why didn't you go home?"

Uriah replied to David, "The Chest **[also called the Ark of the Covenant—it represents the presence of God]** is out there with the fighting men of Israel and Judah—in tents. My master Joab and his servants are roughing it out in the fields. So, how can I go home and eat and drink and enjoy my wife? On your life, I'll not do it!"

. . . In the morning David wrote a letter to Joab and sent it with Uriah. In the letter he wrote, "Put Uriah in the front lines where the fighting is the fiercest. Then pull back and leave him exposed so that he's sure to be killed." **[Low down and nasty!]**

Verse-atility: Loving God, wipe away my wrongs.

So Joab, holding the city under siege, put Uriah in a place where he knew there were fierce enemy fighters. When the city's defenders came out to fight Joab, some of David's soldiers were killed, including Uriah the Hittite.

. . . When Uriah's wife heard that her husband was dead, she grieved for her husband. When the time of mourning was over, David sent someone to bring her to his house. She became his wife and bore him a son.

But God was not at all pleased with what David had done, and sent Nathan to David. Nathan said to him, "There were two men in the same city—one rich, the other poor. The rich man had huge flocks of sheep, herds of cattle. The poor man had nothing but one little female lamb, which he had bought and raised. It grew up with him and his children as a member of the family. It ate off his plate and drank from his cup and slept on his bed. It was like a daughter to him.

"One day a traveler dropped in on the rich man. He was too stingy to take an animal from his own herds or flocks to make a meal for his visitor, so he took the poor man's lamb and prepared a meal to set before his guest."

David exploded in anger. "As surely as God lives," he said to Nathan, "the man who did this ought to be lynched! He must repay for the lamb four times over for his crime and his stinginess!"

"You're the man!" said Nathan. **[You can run but you can't hide!]**

Permission is granted by Standard Publishing to reproduce this **Outtakes** handout for ministry purposes only (not for resale).

7 Mean Girl

Director's Commentary

NOW SHOWING: *Mean Girl*
FROM THE BIBLE: Jezebel steals Naboth's vineyard (1 Kings 21:1-19).
RATED PG-13 FOR: forgery of documents, theft, and murder
POV: Making a wrong action look right doesn't make it right.
KEY VERSE: "The integrity of the upright guides them, but the unfaithful are destroyed by their duplicity" (Proverbs 11:3).

The Lesson	Time	What you'll do...	How you'll do it...	What you'll need...
Take 1: Preview	15 to 20 minutes	Start off your lesson by introducing the theme with a relational, creative activity.	Option 1: Students act out "The In Crowd" drama and discuss it.	5 photocopies of "The In Crowd" script (pp. 100, 101); markers, group journal supplies (*Optional:* items from your prop box; department store shopping bags, lip gloss, a bottle of perfume, movie snacks)
			Option 2: Students watch a DVD version of "The In Crowd" and discuss it. Or, choose to do both.	*Shocking and Scandalous Stories from the Bible DVD*, TV and DVD player; group journal supplies
Take 2: Feature Presentation	15 to 20 minutes	Dive into the Bible story and explore it together.	Small group and large group discussion	Photocopies of **Outtakes** (p. 102); green paper, markers, scissors, twine or yarn, tape *Optional:* Bibles
Take 3: Critics' Corner	15 to 20 minutes	Help your students grasp God's point of view and wrap things up with a fun team-building activity.	Discussion, game, and prayer	Photocopies of **Outtakes** (p. 102); group journal; index cards, markers, bag of treats (*Optional:* timer)

Why Is This PG-13 Story in the Bible?

Ahab, prince of Israel, and Jezebel, princess of Phoenicia, don't marry for love. Their marriage seals a political alliance. Introducing their story, 1 Kings 16:30 says Ahab did more evil than all those who came before him, and the book of Revelation points to a woman named Jezebel as the ultimate description of someone who rejects God to the core (Revelation 2:20). They don't come more evil than that.

As king, Ahab is a competent leader, but he's spineless when it comes to his tyrannical wife. She wants to promote worship of a false god, and Ahab goes along. In exchange, it becomes clear he can count on her to get him what he wants.

One thing Ahab wants is a vineyard in Jezreel—or more precisely, the land. The capital of Israel at the time is Samaria, but Ahab has a summer palace in Jezreel and he wants to grow vegetables. The problem is, Naboth owns the land and it's not for sale—not for any price. Naboth won't sell his family's inheritance. First Kings 21:4 tells us Ahab "went to bed, stuffed his face in a pillow, and refused to eat" (*The Message*). Now that's a royal sulk! Enter Jezebel, who doesn't know the meaning of "no, thank you."

Jezebel has no use for Hebrew religion or law—unless it's to her advantage. Someone who blasphemes God can be stoned, so she arranges to have Naboth framed. It takes two witnesses, so she makes sure there are two accusers. A call for fasting implies looming disaster unless the sinner who has brought judgment on the people is removed, so she orders a fast and makes sure Naboth is the sinner. In an abuse of power, Jezebel makes it look as if everything is by the book and delivers the land to Ahab without remorse.

God sends the prophet Elijah to confront Ahab. Though Jezebel did the scheming, Ahab is complicit; he let his rage toward Naboth rise to the point of condoning murder. God tells Ahab dogs will lick up his blood—which happens later when Ahab dies (see 1 Kings 22:37, 38).

> **Connecting with Community**
> Log on to www.shockingandscandalous.com to connect with other ministries:
> - Check out a sample video of other students in action.
> - Share with other leaders at the PG-13 forum about what's working in your ministry, what's not, or how you used *Shocking and Scandalous* this week.
> - Or ask for input about other aspects of middle school ministry.

SHOCKING AND SCANDALOUS STORIES FROM THE BIBLE

This Bible story will help middle schoolers understand that it's not enough to be committed to something; it's *where* that commitment lies that makes the difference.

Take It to Your Students

Here are some key points to put in front of your students with this lesson:
- No matter how powerful the evil, God still determines right and wrong.
- Convincing yourself that something is right when it's not will get you nowhere.
- Motives tell the truth, even when actions seem acceptable. ✗

Mean Girl: The Lesson

Take 1: Preview (15 to 20 minutes)

Setup: This activity will set up the day's Bible story in a relational way as students discuss a skit in which a popular clique elicits help to pull off a party.

Set design: Create a relaxed atmosphere for *Preview*. Ask students to sit on the floor in a circle on pillows, seat cushions, or colorful mats. The drama will be performed in the middle. Popcorn or movie snacks will help set a movie mood.

Makeup and effects: For today's drama, consider having students select props and costumes from your one-size-fits-all prop box.

Props: Supplies for the journal option you've chosen, markers; 5 copies of the "The In Crowd" skit (pp. 100, 101)

(*Optional:* items from your prop box, department store shopping bags, lip gloss, a bottle of perfume, movie snacks for your audience)

QUIET ON THE SET

To launch the lesson:
- Welcome everyone to the group. Use first names or preferred nicknames and introduce visitors. After your students have had some time to socialize, pull them in and have them get comfortable.
- Go over your Rules of Engagement, if needed. (See the Rules of Engagement suggestions on p. 6 for more information.)

- Review the journaling component you've chosen for your group. (See Create a Group Journal on p. 10 for more information.)

ACTION

Either have students perform the "The In Crowd" skit, watch "The In Crowd" on the *Shocking and Scandalous Stories from the Bible DVD*, or do both. If you choose to have students perform the skit live, give copies of the script to the actors and have them prep by reading through their parts once or twice. Also, invite actors to rummage through the prop box for items to enhance their performance.

> If you want, make a video of your students' live performance. Play it back later (perhaps for the entire church).

PLAY BACK

Discuss "The In Crowd" with your group using the suggestions below as your guide. As usual, don't edit your students' responses—allow them to discuss freely. In the journaling option you've chosen, have a volunteer record the group's overall impressions and Sasha's possible response to Ana's invitation to come to her house. Be sure to jot "The In Crowd" and today's date at the top of the journal entry.

Are you in or out? What would you do to be part of the "in" crowd? It's a decision you may make a hundred times this year—at school, with friends, on the field, online, or on your cell phone.

Use these questions to get the discussion going:

- **What feelings do you think Sasha's experiencing?** *(Embarrassment, frustration, nervousness, worry, excitement)*
- **In your opinion, what qualities make a good friend? How many of those qualities do we see demonstrated in today's skit?**
- **Have you ever been tricked by somebody else's dishonesty? Explain.**
- **How far would *you* go not to feel left out?**

Dishonesty is a lie, even when it's gift-wrapped to look like something else. Today's Bible story is Oscar-worthy in this regard! Up next: disbelief, deception, and death in *Mean Girl*. ✘

Take 2: Feature Presentation (15 to 20 minutes)

Setup: Your students will take a close look at the story of Jezebel stealing Naboth's land and discuss making wrong actions look right.

Props: Photocopies of **Outtakes** (p. 102); green paper, markers, scissors, twine or yarn, tape

Optional: Bibles

QUIET ON THE SET

Pass out copies of **Outtakes**, one per student. *Optional:* Have students grab their own Bibles.

> Just a reminder that we've included examples of possible student answers to some of the discussion questions in these lessons. You'll see them in *italics.* If your students get stuck on a question, share one of the sample answers to help them get their discussion started.

ACTION

Use **Outtakes** to introduce and teach the Bible story. First, briefly introduce the **Cast** and make sure your students know who's who. Next, use **Movie Trailer** to cover the highlights of the Bible background and story. Then read the Bible story (1 Kings 21:1-19) out loud from **Outtakes** or have a volunteer read it. If you prefer, ask students to read from their own Bibles.

PLAY BACK

Divide your group into two or more small teams for discussion with an adult or older teen leader for each group. If possible, plan to make the groups all guys or all girls. Guys will look more closely at Ahab and Elijah (Guy Talk), and girls will explore Jezebel's point of view (Girl Talk). Remind group leaders to be ready to enhance discussion with insights from **Why Is This PG-13 Story in the Bible?** (p. 91).

Give each group a supply of green paper, scissors, and markers. Have students discuss the motivations they see in the story characters; as they do, they should write their thoughts on pieces of green paper that they've cut into the shape of leaves.

What in the world were Jezebel and Ahab thinking? Let's find out. Cut some leaves from the paper and write down what you think was going on in their heads.

Guy Talk: Get into the heads of Ahab and Elijah.

- Ahab offered to pay for the land—so was it wrong for him to want it? Why or why not? *(Duh! It belonged to someone else. Naboth said no.)*
- What does Ahab's tendency to sulk tell you about him? *(He wants his own way.)*
- Does Ahab bear any responsibility for Jezebel's plan to steal and murder? Make your case. *(Yes—he let it happen, even though he had to know it was wrong.)*
- In your opinion, what was the hardest part about Elijah's job? *(Standing up to the king.)*

Girl Talk: Get into the head of Jezebel.

- What do you think is Jezebel's opinion of her husband? How does she view him? *(He was weak; he didn't act like a king.)*
- Do you think Jezebel cares about the vineyard? Why or why not? *(She probably doesn't. She just wants to prove she can push people around. She's proving a point to Ahab.)*
- Do you see anything at all to admire in Jezebel as a woman? Explain.
- In your opinion, what matters most to Jezebel? *(Getting her own way. Making people do what she wanted.)*

Bring the groups back together and briefly review discussion results. Together, create a "vineyard" with the leaves by taping them to a wall and using twine or yarn to create an underlying vine.

Continue your discussion with questions like:

- What's your opinion of the people in this story? Why?
- Ahab and Jezebel would be hard-pressed to argue they honestly believed forgery, stealing, and murder were right. How did they justify what they were doing?
- Why do you think this story about stealing and murder is in the Bible? *(This is a good time to remind your students of today's Key Verse: "The integrity of the upright guides them, but the unfaithful are destroyed by their duplicity" [Proverbs 11:3].)*

Can you spot the phony? Jezebel had no sense of right and wrong. And she topped it off with a bittersweet frosting to make it look like she was doing nothing wrong.

Use these questions to prompt more large-group discussion:
- **Where in the story could the characters have made better choices?**
- **How did the choices the characters made hurt other people?**
- **How might the story have been different if Ahab had a spine? If Jezebel had a conscience? If Elijah were a coward?**

We can convince ourselves that what we're doing is OK. We might even convince our friends. But making a wrong action look right doesn't make it right. Period. ✘

Take 3: Critics' Corner (15 to 20 minutes)

Setup: Reinforce the points you want your students to take away from today's lesson.

Props: Group journal with entries from Take 1; **Outtakes** handout (p. 102); index cards (10 per team of 3 to 5 students), markers, timer or clock, bag of treats

QUIET ON THE SET

Grab the group journal and ask students to gather to review the "The In Crowd" entries recorded during Take 1.

ACTION

Consider the POV

Have a volunteer read the group journal entries from the opening discussion about the "The In Crowd" skit, then ask:

- **How important is honesty to you? Explain.**
- **Based on the POV, what should Sasha's final decision be? Why?**

Have a volunteer read aloud today's **POV** from **Outtakes**: *Making a wrong action look right doesn't make it right.*

We, too, are tempted to twist the truth to get what we want. Consider today's POV and these questions the next time you need to decide: "Am I in . . . or out?"

Jot the following five questions in the group journal where students can revisit them in the weeks to come.

7: Mean Girl

"The In Crowd" Questions
Why do I want to be included in this activity?
Will this activity hurt me or others?
Will I get into trouble?
What would my parents say?
What does the Bible say?

> If time allows, have students pair up to brainstorm and discuss situations they might face in which the "The In Crowd" questions could help them make a good decision.

Understand God's Truth

Jezebel used trickery to get what she wanted . . . and won—in her eyes. But no matter how powerful the evil, God sees it for what it is. "The integrity of the upright guides them, but the unfaithful are destroyed by their duplicity" (Proverbs 11:3).

Ask the group:

- **What have we learned from today's story?** *(Two-faced Jezebel lies, cheats, and kills to get Naboth's vineyard. Making actions look right doesn't make them right.)*
- **When is the truth not the truth?** *(When even a tiny bit of it is a lie!)*

Doing right says a lot about you. It says to friends and others that you're a person of integrity. That's an honorable and very good thing.

Teamwork

We can help each other stand strong when it's tough to do what's right. Be young men and women of integrity this week, committed to God and to each other.

PLAY BACK

Wrap up the meeting with a team-building game that gives students a sense of what integrity really looks like. Then close in prayer.

Integrity Challenge

Needed: index cards (10 per team), markers, bag of treats
(Optional: timer)
Goal: Work quickly to complete different tasks using "integrity cards."

How to Play:

Have students sit in a large circle and brainstorm together all the positive traits that make them outstanding children of God! Aim to create a lengthy verbal list.

If your students need help, toss out some of these ideas. Examples of positive attributes include the fruit of the Spirit: being loving, joyous, peaceful, patient, kind, good, faithful, fair, gentle, self-controlled. Other attributes or traits include being able, accepting, assured, artistic, adventurous, brave, bold, cheerful, calm, committed, considerate, creative, confident, devoted, disciplined, dynamic, eager, energetic, engaging, enthusiastic, forgiving, friendly, gentle, glad, grateful, gracious, happy, hard-working, helpful, honest, hopeful, humble, imaginative, (having) integrity, indispensable, irreplaceable, instrumental, (seeking) justice, jubilant, lovable, loyal, moral, nice, patient, positive, reliable, respectful, responsible, sincere, thankful, thoughtful, tolerant, trusting, understanding, warm, and so on.

When you're done brainstorming, break up your group into smaller team circles of three to five students. Hand ten index cards and a marker to a volunteer in each circle.

Give teams the following instructions, allowing time for them to finish each task before going on to the next one.

Task 1: On your index cards, write ten positive traits that begin with the first ten letters of the alphabet, one word per card. You have one minute. Ready, set, *go!* (When teams are done, have them read their words aloud for the rest of the groups to hear.)

Task 2: Swap cards with another circle. Scatter cards on the floor. Then place your new cards in reverse alphabetical order. You have 15 seconds. Ready, set, *go!*

Task 3: Swap cards with another circle again and scatter your new cards on the floor. Then have each person pick his or her favorite word card. Write positive trait words for each letter of the word on your card. You have one minute. Ready, set, *go!* (When teams are done with this task, have students read the new positive traits they wrote to the rest of their team members.)

Task 4: Swap cards one last time. Now work as a team to build a house of cards! The first house standing wins.

You be the judge! The team that worked the fastest and with the most integrity wins a candy treat.

After the game, say: **"The integrity of the upright guides them, but the unfaithful are destroyed by their duplicity" (Proverbs 11:3). Recognize the reward of making great, positive choices, and commit to doing right.**

Close with Prayer

God is trying to tell you something!

Ask your group to look again at **Outtakes** and repeat today's **Key Verse:** "The integrity of the upright guides them, but the unfaithful are destroyed by their duplicity" (Proverbs 11:3). Then point out this week's *Verse-atility: I'll work at being honest even when others don't.* Encourage your students to keep God's truth front and center in their lives this week. If time permits, jot the verse (or *Verse-atility*) in the group journal and have everyone initial it.

> **Verse-atility**: *I'll work at being honest even when others don't.*

Invite students to share prayer requests. Then pray with an upbeat message of how honesty is a joyful treasure we give others, a reassurance to those we love. ✘

The In Crowd

Characters:
NARRATOR
JOLENE, ANA, and TORI: three "cool" eighth-grade girls
SASHA: perhaps a little naïve, but a good-hearted seventh-grade girl
Scene: The fragrance counter at a department store
Prop Suggestions: Select any props or costumes you want from the prop box. Also, if you want, use department store shopping bags, lip gloss, and a bottle of perfume (or just pretend!).

SCRIPT

NARRATOR:
Sasha recognizes the eighth-grade girls at the store counter. They're looking at jewelry and talking about what would go best with their new outfits. Jolene is Sasha's neighbor. She runs up to say hello.

SASHA:
(smiling, breathless from running over) **Hi Jolene!**

(Jolene acts like she's not sure who this girl is . . .)

It's Sasha . . . I live down the street from you.

JOLENE:
Uh . . . hi. How's it going?

SASHA:
(lifts up her full shopping bags) **Great! I've been shopping with my birthday money.**

(Jolene, Ana, and Tori smirk. It's clear all three girls aren't interested in talking with Sasha.)

JOLENE:
(glancing at Sasha, then turning away) **That's nice.**

(The girls turn away, ignoring Sasha, looking at jewelry or spraying on perfume)

ANA:
So, we need a room to store all the stuff we collect for the canned food drive, right? We could probably use Mr. Jackson's room to sort everything. *(gets a mischievous look on her face)* **And then . . . what if we have a little *fun* afterward? Mr. Jackson doesn't have to know.**

TORI:
(nodding) **It might work.**

SASHA:
What're you guys talking about?

TORI:
(turning slowly to acknowledge Sasha) **Well, if you have to know, we're planning a little party.**

SASHA:
That's cool. I've been thinking about planning something too.

ANA:
(absent-mindedly) **Yeah, what?**

SASHA:
(excited) **A club. For the Christian kids at our school.**

(Tori and Jolene turn to each other and giggle.)

ANA:
A *Christian club*? *(laughing just a bit)* Are you *serious*?

SASHA:
Yeah. It could be a fun way to get to know other Christian kids, and it could really help us grow in our faith. I was thinking it could be like one of those clubs for athletes—and we could invite professional Christian athletes to come talk to us. They could tell us how to set goals and stuff—and stay in God's Word.

JOLENE:
(now she turns to face Sasha) Look, nothing personal, but that sounds really lame.

SASHA:
(somewhat defensively) Well, I was also thinking about joining the track team next spring. . . . It sounds pretty fun.

ANA:
(snobbily) Track? That's not as cool as you think. And your club sounds like some sort of "Be all you can be!" commercial or something.

JOLENE:
(rolling her eyes) Seriously.

NARRATOR:
Sasha feels stupid for having mentioned the club at all.

TORI:
(fake yawning, giving a mean look to Sasha) I'm bored.

ANA:
(gathering her shopping bags, texting on cell phone) Let's go.

(Sasha looks hurt, but says nothing.)

ANA:
(Almost an afterthought) Uh, see ya around, Sasha.

(Ana, Jolene, and Tori walk away.)

JOLENE:
(with some distance, she says to the others) Sasha looks like she wants to come with us *so* bad. She's so desperate. . . . Like that will ever happen!

ANA:
(scheming) You know . . . *(deep thought going on)* Sasha might be just what we need for our party. Her older brother knows a bunch of hot guys.

(The three girls all have the same look on their faces.)

TORI:
You're brilliant, Ana.

ANA:
(turning toward Sasha—with a fake smile) Hey, Sasha, wanna come to my house?

NARRATOR:
Sasha could take a hint—but now comes this invite. Insane! But . . . it wouldn't hurt to be seen with Ana; she knows everybody. What's a girl to do? What would you do if you were in Sasha's place? Do you think Ana's invitation is sincere? Would you accept it?

(Skit ends; actors rejoin group.)

Permission is granted by Standard Publishing to reproduce this "The In Crowd" script for ministry purposes only (not for resale).

Outtakes

CAST

Ahab: king of Israel
Jezebel: Ahab's foreign wife, a worshiper of Baal
Naboth: owns a vineyard
Elijah: prophet of God

MOVIE TRAILER

- Ahab wants Naboth's vineyard to use for a garden, but Naboth doesn't want to sell it to him.
- Jezebel sets out to get the vineyard no matter what.
- Jezebel arranges for people to accuse Naboth of things he didn't do.
- Because of the false accusations, Naboth is killed. Jezebel takes the vineyard.
- God sends Elijah to confront Ahab about his sin.

Verse-atility:
I'll work at being honest even when others don't.

POV: Making a wrong action look right doesn't make it right.
Key Verse: The integrity of the upright guides them, but the unfaithful are destroyed by their duplicity (Proverbs 11:3).

MEAN GIRL

1 Kings 21:1-19 *(The Message) (We've added a few of our own comments **in bold** below.)*

Naboth the Jezreelite owned a vineyard in Jezreel that bordered the palace of Ahab king of Samaria. One day Ahab spoke to Naboth, saying, "Give me your vineyard so I can use it as a kitchen garden; it's right next to my house—so convenient. In exchange I'll give you a far better vineyard, or if you'd prefer I'll pay you money for it."

But Naboth told Ahab, "Not on your life! So help me God, I'd never sell the family farm to you!" **[Food fight—almost . . .]** Ahab went home in a black mood, sulking over Naboth the Jezreelite's words, "I'll never turn over my family inheritance to you." He went to bed, stuffed his face in his pillow, and refused to eat.

Jezebel his wife came to him. She said, "What's going on? Why are you so out of sorts and refusing to eat?"

He told her, "Because I spoke to Naboth the Jezreelite. I said, 'Give me your vineyard—I'll pay you for it or, if you'd rather, I'll give you another vineyard in exchange.' And he said, 'I'll never give you my vineyard.'"

Jezebel said, "Is this any way for a king of Israel to act? Aren't you the boss? On your feet! Eat! Cheer up! I'll take care of this; I'll get the vineyard of this Naboth the Jezreelite for you."

She **[Mean Girl]** wrote letters over Ahab's signature, stamped them with his official seal, and sent them to the elders in Naboth's city and to the civic leaders. She wrote "Call for a fast day and put Naboth at the head table. Then seat a couple of stool pigeons across from him who, in front of everybody will say, 'You! You blasphemed God and the king!' Then they'll throw him out and stone him to death."

And they did it. The men of the city—the elders and civic leaders **[Warning. Warning. SCAM ALERT!]**—followed Jezebel's instructions that she wrote in the letters sent to them. They called for a fast day and seated Naboth at the head table. Then they brought in two stool pigeons and seated them opposite Naboth. In front of everybody the two degenerates accused him, "He blasphemed God and the king!" The company threw him out in the street, stoned him mercilessly, and he died. **[Headline: "Mean Girl Gossip Leads to Gruesome Death."]**

When Jezebel got word that Naboth had been stoned to death, she told Ahab, "Go for it, Ahab—take the vineyard of Naboth the Jezreelite for your own, the vineyard he refused to sell you. Naboth is no more; Naboth is dead."

The minute Ahab heard that Naboth was dead, he set out for the vineyard of Naboth the Jezreelite and claimed it for his own.

Then God stepped in and spoke to Elijah the Tishbite, "On your feet; go down and confront Ahab of Samaria, king of Israel. You'll find him in the vineyard of Naboth; he's gone there to claim it as his own. Say this to him: 'God's word: What's going on here? First murder, then theft?' Then tell him, 'God's verdict: The very spot where the dogs lapped up Naboth's blood, they'll lap up your blood—that's right, *your* blood.'" **[Breaking it down as only God can!]**

Permission is granted by Standard Publishing to reproduce **Outtakes** for ministry purposes only (not for resale).

Her Majesty's Secret Service

Director's Commentary

NOW SHOWING: *Her Majesty's Secret Service*

FROM THE BIBLE: Esther stands up for her people (Esther 3:5, 6, 8, 9; 7:1-10).

RATED PG-13 FOR: a horrific plot to destroy the Jewish people by genocide

POV: With God's strength, you can stand up against what you know is wrong.

KEY VERSE: "There is no wisdom, no insight, no plan that can succeed against the Lord" (Proverbs 21:30).

The Lesson	Time	What you'll do . . .	How you'll do it . . .	What you'll need . . .
Take 1: Preview	15 to 20 minutes	Start off your lesson by introducing the theme with a relational, creative activity.	Option 1: Students perform on-the-spot improvs, then talk about the challenges of doing the right thing.	Group journal supplies; 1 photocopy of "Middle School Confidential" (pp. 112, 113), cut into slips; prop box
			Option 2: Students watch a DVD version of "Middle School Confidential" and discuss it. Or, choose to do both.	*Shocking and Scandalous Stories from the Bible DVD*, TV and DVD player
Take 2: Feature Presentation	15 to 20 minutes	Dive into the Bible story and explore it together.	Small group and large group discussion	Photocopies of **Outtakes** (p. 116); markers, large index cards (or pieces of poster board) *Optional:* Bibles
Take 3: Critics' Corner	15 to 20 minutes	Help your students grasp God's point of view and wrap things up with a fun team-building activity.	Discussion, game, and prayer	Photocopies of **Outtakes** (p. 116); group journal; photocopies of the "We're All in This Together" handout (pp. 114, 115), pens or markers

Why Is This PG-13 Story in the Bible?

How did a nice Jewish girl end up being queen of Persia?

In the sixth century BC, prominent citizens of Jerusalem were hauled into captivity in Babylon. About five decades later, Persia conquered Babylon, and a few years after that, the Persian king allowed Jews to return to their land if they wished. However, in the intervening years, many Jews had become settled in Persia, running their own businesses and building a good life, so not everyone returned to Jerusalem. Esther was part of a family that remained in Persia.

When King Xerxes's wife Vashti defies him, he banishes her. An expansive compulsory beauty contest (to find a replacement for the queen) turns up the charming, delightful Esther, who wins the honor of marrying the king (whether she likes it or not!). Even as queen, Esther cannot speak to her husband unless he asks for her. It's a delicate balance, and when Esther's cousin Mordecai crosses Haman, the king's second-in-command, it all nearly topples.

Haman is egotistical and ambitious, and he isn't about to let Mordecai stand in his way. When Haman demands that people bow to him, Mordecai refuses; he will bow only to God. Incensed, Haman hatches a plan to wipe out not only Mordecai, but all the Jewish people of the Persian kingdom. Xerxes blindly trusts Haman to make these strategic decisions, plus Haman assures the king the enterprise will yield a hefty increase to the royal bottom line.

> **Connecting with Community**
> Log on to www.shockingandscandalous.com to connect with other ministries:
> - Check out a sample video of other students in action.
> - Share with other leaders at the PG-13 forum about what's working in your ministry, what's not, or how you used *Shocking and Scandalous* this week.
> - Or ask for input about other aspects of middle school ministry.

What Haman is doing is wrong, and Mordecai is not going to take it sitting down. He launches his secret weapon: Esther, whom no one in the palace realizes is a Jew. Esther could keep her secret and preserve her own life. She could say she couldn't do anything about this problem. She actually does say, "I could get killed for approaching the king!" But in the end, she rallies the Jews to pray for her and squares off with the injustice.

Esther plans carefully. She softens up the king with a couple of satiating dinners. At the right moment, she identifies herself as a Jew and turns the spotlight on Haman as the man who would kill the queen. Exit Haman—via the gallows.

8: Her Majesty's Secret Service

This story is historical. Real people stood up against real evil. This Bible story helps middle schoolers see they don't have to be passive when authority is being abused and used for evil reasons. Like Esther and Mordecai, they can take a stand for what's right.

Take It to Your Students

Here are some key points to put in front of your students with this lesson:
- When you see injustice, you can do something about it.
- Doing the right thing might take you out of your comfort zone.
- You can stand up for what's right with God's strength. ✗

Her Majesty's Secret Service: The Lesson

Take 1: Preview (15 to 20 minutes)

Setup: This activity will set up the day's Bible story in a relational way as students role-play challenges they face when trying to do the right thing at school.

Set design: Create a flexible space for performers; performers and audience will switch places often.

Makeup and effects: Pull out your one-size-fits-all prop box for students to rummage through to enhance their role-plays.

Props: The journal option you've chosen, markers; 1 photocopy of "Middle School Confidential" (pp. 112, 113) cut into slips, prop box
Option 2: Shocking and Scandalous Stories from the Bible DVD, TV, and DVD player

QUIET ON THE SET

To launch the lesson:
- Welcome everyone to the group. Use first names or preferred nicknames and introduce visitors. After your students have had some time to socialize, pull them in and have them get comfortable.
- Go over your Rules of Engagement, if needed. (See the Rules of Engagement suggestions on p. 6 for more information.)

- Review the journaling component you've chosen for your group. (See Create a Group Journal on p. 10 for more information.)

ACTION

DVD Option: Start this activity by showing your group "Middle School Confidential" from the *Shocking and Scandalous Stories from the Bible DVD* before students start this activity. (The video shows youth group students doing only two of the five listed scenarios, so you can try different ones, re-do the same to see if your students can do them better, or try all five.)

Say: **"Middle School Confidential" is a new Reality TV show filming in a school near you!**

Have students form trios, then explain that they're about to improvise role-play scenarios showing the "producer" (you!) the challenges middle school students face in doing the right thing during a typical school day.

Call trios up front, one at a time. Give the performing trio one of the sets of slips from the "Middle School Confidential" handout. Have trio members read their assigned scenario out loud to the large group. Then have each member of the trio pick one of the slips—that's their assigned character. (If you've got more than five trios, you'll need to repeat some of the scenarios.)

Remember, this is improv! Give the performing trios one minute to read their slips and get into their roles. Invite them to use items from the prop box if they want, then have them act out their scenario any way they'd like.

Repeat this process with each trio—allowing just one minute for them to read their assigned roles and scenario before they improv in front of everyone else.

PLAY BACK

Applaud performances! Spend time discussing the improvs with your group; also, invite students to comment about some of their own experiences. Have a volunteer enter the date and title ("Middle School Confidential") in the group journal and jot down the group's reaction to each improv. Encourage all students to participate with the journal, even if it is just to initial entries in agreement.

Bad day alert! It's hard to do right when others work against you.

8: Her Majesty's Secret Service

Use these questions to get the discussion going:
- **How did the role-plays make you feel? Why?**
- **What bothered you the most?**
- **How do you respond to situations like this at school?**
- **Have you ever come to the rescue of somebody else? If so, share your story.**

Let's pump up the pressure. What if your entire school needed *you* to do the right thing in a tough spot—but it might cost you your life? This week's four-star PG-13 feature documents a beauty queen—the fairest in all the land—who faces a similar choice. *Her Majesty's Secret Service* is up next. ✘

Take 2: Feature Presentation (15 to 20 minutes)

Setup: Your students will take a close look at the story of Esther and discuss standing up against what they know is wrong.

Props: Photocopies of **Outtakes** (p. 116); markers, large index cards (or pieces of poster board)

Optional: Bibles

> You may want to supplement the discussion of the passages on **Outtakes** by also reading Esther 4:12-16 out loud to your group.

QUIET ON THE SET

Pass out copies of **Outtakes**, one per student. *Optional:* Have students grab their own Bibles.

ACTION

Use **Outtakes** to introduce and teach the Bible story. First, briefly introduce the **Cast** and make sure your students know who's who. Next, use **Movie Trailer** to cover the highlights of the Bible background and story. Then read the Bible story (Esther 3:5, 6, 8, 9; 7:1-10) out loud from **Outtakes** or have a volunteer read. If you prefer, ask students to read the passage aloud from their own Bibles.

> Just a reminder that we've got some helpful insights about forming small groups in the Team Talk Small Groups section on pp. 10, 11.

PLAY BACK

Divide your group into two or more small teams for discussion with an adult or older teen leader for each group. If possible, make the groups all guys and all girls. Guys will look more closely at Haman and Mordecai (Guy Talk), and girls will step into Esther's shoes (Girl Talk). Remind small group leaders to be ready to enhance discussion with insights from **Why Is This PG-13 Story in the Bible?** (p. 104).

Give each small group a stack of index cards (or posters) and markers. Explain that groups should answer the discussion questions by writing "cue cards"—a complete sentence reflecting something the character would say.

> Consider making a video of your students' improv role-plays. Play it back later (perhaps for the entire church).

The story of Queen Esther is one of high drama, not drama queen. Let's bring the story to light in our groups.

Guy Talk: Get into the heads of Haman and Mordecai.

- **Mordecai: What I don't like about Haman is . . .** *(Arrogant; abuses power)*
- **Haman: What I hate about Mordecai is . . .** *(Won't bow to me; thinks he's too good to follow orders; thinks he's holy)*
- **Mordecai: Haman's problem is . . .** *(A big head; a messed-up idea of who's in charge)*
- **Haman: Mordecai thinks he's . . .** *(More important than he is; so smart)*

Girl Talk: Get into the head of Esther.

- **I'm afraid because . . .** *(I'm a woman; I have no real power; I could die.)*
- **I hope my husband will . . .** *(Do the right thing; save my life; save my people; get rid of Haman.)*
- **It's hard to know what to do because . . .** *(It's dangerous; I might fail; I might die.)*
- **I'm doing this because . . .** *(It's the right thing.)*

Bring everybody back together and review discussion results by having volunteers assume character roles and read their cue cards aloud for the large group.

Continue your discussion as a large group by asking questions like:

- **What titles would you suggest for this drama? Why?**

8: Her Majesty's Secret Service

- In your opinion, what were the true motivations of the characters in this story?
- Why do you think this story about intent to kill and possible genocide is in the Bible? *(This is an opportunity to remind students of today's Key Verse: "There is no wisdom, no insight, no plan that can succeed against the Lord" [Proverbs 21:30].)*

Haman's hatred for the Jews grew from pride. He plotted carefully to kill them, but, as we've read, Esther planned just as carefully to save them. God protected his people. He is the one true God.

Ask the group questions like:
- What choices could Haman have made differently that would have changed the story?
- What key choices did Mordecai make? How about Esther?

> Some of your students may know the larger story of Esther. Encourage them to use their Bibles to draw on other parts of the story during discussion times if they wish.

It would be an uphill battle and Mordecai knew it. Yet, Esther took it on and risked her crown to save her people. With God's strength, she stood against what she knew was wrong. So can you. ✘

Take 3: Critics' Corner (15 to 20 minutes)

Set up: Reinforce the points you want your students to take away from today's lesson.
Props: Group journal with entries from Take 1; **Outtakes** (p. 116); photocopies of the "We're All in This Together" handout (pp. 114, 115) (1 per student), pens or markers

> If one of your groups has just two students, join in yourself or recruit another student who's already acted to join in and do another improv.

QUIET ON THE SET

Grab the group journal and ask students to review the "Middle School Confidential" role-play entries.

SHOCKING AND SCANDALOUS STORIES FROM THE BIBLE

ACTION

Consider the POV

Ask the group:

- Describe the ultimate rescuer. What would he or she be like?
- Now see *yourself* as the ultimate rescuer. How does the role fit? Explain.

> To encourage honest and open discussion, consider having students form pairs to talk about these three discussion questions.

- Will helping someone today help you be a better person ten years from now? Explain.

Draw students' attention to the **POV** on the **Outtakes** handout: *With God's strength, you can stand up against what you know is wrong.* Then invite students to complete the following sentence:

- I know this to be true about today's POV: _____.

Read over earlier entries in the group journal one more time, inviting the group to discuss:

- How could the outcomes we recorded become more successful experiences in the future? *(Become a prayer warrior; seek guidance from those in the know—parents, siblings, teachers; be an ultimate rescuer for another.)*

Jot new insights in the journal.

Understand God's Truth

Today's Bible story took place in a time and culture that could have cared less about God or his chosen people. Yet, the God we love and serve today protected them.

Ask the group:

- What have we learned from today's story? *(With godly courage, Esther puts a stop to the soon-to-be slaughter of her people.)*
- Being a member of God's kingdom requires us to live outside of our comfort zones. What are *you* willing to risk to help others? Rejection? Embarrassment? Something worse? Explain.

You've learned you can come to the rescue of others. With God's strength, be prepared to stand against what you know is wrong.

Teamwork

We respect each other. We are a strong group. Let's support each other through difficult times at school this week with a phone call, text, or just a great talk. A little encouragement can go a long way as we aim to courageously make right choices.

8: Her Majesty's Secret Service

PLAY BACK

Wrap up the meeting with a team-building game that helps participants get to know each other better and form stronger bonds as a group. Then close in prayer.

We're All in This Together

Needed: photocopies of "We're All In This Together" (pp. 114, 115), 1 per student; pens or markers

Goal: Use the handout to identify the various skills, talents, and interests of group members.

> **Verse-atility:** *Even on its best day, evil can't outsmart God.*

How to Play:

Say: **Teams that know each other well can do outstanding work for God. So, who's up for *Operation: Join the Club*?**

Distribute pens or markers and copies of "We're All in This Together," one per student. Have students circulate and find classmates to initial a behavior or skill that reflects them on the sheet. Challenge them with this rule: Students can only initial *one* item on a given handout.

> If you've got less than twenty people participating in this activity, allow students to initial two (or three) items on a sheet.

Close with Prayer

No matter how powerful the evil, God determines right and wrong. Remember, it's not enough to be committed to something. It needs to be the *right* thing.

Ask your group to look again at **Outtakes** and repeat today's **Key Verse**: "There is no wisdom, no insight, no plan that can succeed against the Lord" (Proverbs 21:30). Then point out this week's *Verse-atility: Even on its best day, evil can't outsmart God.* If time permits, jot the verse in the group journal and have everyone initial it.

Invite students to share prayer requests, especially those about situations they're facing in school in which they desire the courage and wisdom to do the right thing, and then close in prayer. ✘

Middle School Confidential

BULLYVILLE

Scenario: The three of you meet up in the hallway; below are the three characters you'll be acting out. The eighth-grader bumps into the sixth-grader, maybe on purpose, because he's talking to the cheerleader. How does each of you react?

✂--

Person 1: You're an eighth-grade bully who has had a bad morning. You're used to getting your way. You happen to notice this runty little kid talking to one of the cheerleaders, so you decide maybe you'll give him a little shoulder shiver . . .

✂--

Person 2: You're a sixth-grade math whiz with a crush on the cheerleader whose locker is next to yours. Then this big kid comes by and bumps into you . . .

✂--

You're a seventh-grade cheerleader who tries to be friendly to everybody, and you're extra nice to the sixth-grade math whiz whose locker is next to yours. Then you witness this big kid run into the little one . . .

CHEAT SHEET

Scenario: It's time for the dreaded English class spelling and vocab test—somebody feels tempted to cheat. Here are the three characters who converge on this scene:

✂--

Person 1: You're the class whiz on spelling and vocabulary, and you like to make sure everyone knows it, especially on test days. But as the test begins, you notice something funny happening near you . . .

✂--

Person 2: You meant to study for the spelling and vocab test, but never got around to it (as usual!). You're going to use your usual tricks to make sure you get a decent grade . . .

✂--

Person 3: The kid who never studies always seems to get a better grade on the vocab tests than you do. You suspect cheating, and today's test is your chance to prove it.

TEAM PICKS

Scenario: It's gym class, and it's time to pick teams. These three students (below) collide. What happens next?

✂--

Person 1: You're the class jock who is the captain of every team in gym class. You do whatever it takes to get the players you want on your team.

✂--

Person 2: You're the scrawny kid who never gets picked for anything, but you really like playing sports, and you're pretty good if people would just give you a chance.

✂--

Person 3: You're tall with long arms and everybody expects you to be good at sports, but really you'd rather be reading the latest detective novel.

WANNA HANG OUT?

Scenario: Plans are being made for hanging out over the weekend. These three students wind up at the same table when talk turns to Saturday and Sunday's plans. What happens next?

✂--

Person 1: You're anxious to have your best friend come to your house and see your new video game.

✂--

Person 2: You're that best friend, but also the kind of person who gets along with everyone and will go along with almost anything.

✂--

Person 3: You're the new student at school and seem pretty likeable to most, but you're also still looking for friends. You want to invite someone to go to the movies with you.

TOO CURIOUS?

Scenario: You're all killing time in the hallways between classes when one student makes a grab for another student's backpack. What's going on; what happens next?

✂--

Person 1: You're protective of your backpack because you keep a private diary in there and add to it during the day. You don't like anyone touching your stuff.

✂--

Person 2: You always see the same kid taking a notebook out of his or her backpack and writing stuff. Your curiosity is killing you—you've got to know what that notebook says.

✂--

Person 3: You have a personality that causes you to stick up for the little guy. You don't like to see students picking on other students.

Permission is granted by Standard Publishing to reproduce "Middle School Confidential" for ministry purposes only (not for resale).

We're All in This Together

Directions: Find different people who match these descriptions. When you do, have them initial the box.

loves super-crunchy peanut butter	writes poetry
can whistle the National Anthem (prove it!)	owns a hamster, gerbil, or pet fish
plays soccer or volleyball	has sandals on
can touch knuckles to floor (prove it!)	can recite the Ten Commandments (prove it!)
wears socks with holes (prove it!)	skis

draws original cartoons	wears braces (prove it!)
plays the flute	loves pickles on burgers
can wiggle ears (prove it!)	wants to own a motorcycle
has pierced ears (prove it!)	can yodel (prove it!)
loves super-hot salsa	can moonwalk (prove it!)

Outtakes

CAST
Xerxes: king of Persia
Esther: Jewish young woman who becomes queen
Haman: second-in-command to the king
Mordecai: Esther's cousin, employed at the palace

MOVIE TRAILER
- Haman gets a big head about how important he is and wants everyone to bow to him.
- When Mordecai won't bow to Haman, Haman decides to wipe out the Jews.
- Haman tricks the king into signing a law to kill all the Jews.
- Esther gives the king a dinner party to expose Haman's evil plan—which would include her!
- Angry, the king orders Haman hanged.

Verse-atility: Even on its best day, evil can't outsmart God.

POV: With God's strength, you can stand up against what you know is wrong.

Key Verse: There is no wisdom, no insight, no plan that can succeed against the Lord (Proverbs 21:30).

HER MAJESTY'S SECRET SERVICE
Esther 3:5, 6, 8, 9; 7:1-10 *(The Message)*
*(We've added a few of our own comments in **bold** below.)*

When Haman saw for himself that Mordecai didn't bow down and kneel before him, he was outraged. Meanwhile, having learned that Mordecai was a Jew, Haman hated to waste his fury on just one Jew; he looked for a way to eliminate not just Mordecai but all Jews throughout the whole kingdom of Xerxes.

. . . Haman then spoke with King Xerxes: "There is an odd set of people scattered through the provinces of your kingdom who don't fit in. Their customs and ways are different from those of everybody else. Worse, they disregard the king's laws. They're an affront; the king shouldn't put up with them. If it pleases the king, let orders be given that they be destroyed. I'll pay for it myself. I'll deposit 375 tons of silver in the royal bank to finance the operation." **[Serious motivation!]**

[Mordecai learns of the plot and convinces his cousin Esther to try and stop Haman's plan—even though it means risking her life!]

. . . So the king and Haman went to dinner with Queen Esther. At this second dinner, while they were drinking wine the king again asked, "Queen Esther, what would you like? Half of my kingdom! Just ask and it's yours."

Queen Esther answered, "If I have found favor in your eyes, O King, and if it please the king, give me my life, and give my people lives.

"We've been sold, I and my people, to be destroyed—sold to be massacred, eliminated. If we had just been sold off into slavery, I wouldn't even have brought it up; our troubles wouldn't have been worth bothering the king over."

King Xerxes exploded, "Who? Where is he? This is monstrous!"

"An enemy. An adversary. **[Dum-dum-dum-*dum!*]** This evil Haman," said Esther.

Haman was terror-stricken before the king and queen.

The king, raging, left his wine and stalked out into the palace garden.

Haman stood there pleading with Queen Esther for his life—he could see that the king was finished with him and that he was doomed. As the king came back from the palace garden into the banquet hall, Haman was groveling **[begging!]** at the couch on which Esther reclined. The king roared out, "Will he even molest the queen while I'm just around the corner?"

When that word left the king's mouth, all the blood drained from Haman's face.

Harbona, one of the eunuchs attending the king, spoke up: "Look over there! There's the gallows that Haman had built for Mordecai, who saved the king's life. It's right next to Haman's house—seventy-five feet high!"

The king said, "Hang him on it!" **[Gulp . . .]**

So Haman was hanged on the very gallows that he had built for Mordecai. And the king's hot anger cooled.

*Permission is granted by Standard Publishing to reproduce this **Outtakes** handout for ministry purposes only (not for resale).*

9 Extreme Rampage

Director's Commentary

NOW SHOWING: *Extreme Rampage*

FROM THE BIBLE: Herod kills baby boys in Bethlehem (Matthew 2:1-16).

RATED PG-13 FOR: paranoid rage resulting in infanticide

POV: Emotional reactions cast God's wisdom aside and hurt innocent people.

KEY VERSE: "A fool gives full vent to his anger, but a wise man keeps himself under control" (Proverbs 29:11).

The Lesson	Time	What you'll do . . .	How you'll do it . . .	What you'll need . . .
Take 1: Preview	15 to 20 minutes	Start off your lesson by introducing the theme with a relational, creative activity.	Option 1: Students sketch cartoons and talk about a terrible tyrant.	Photocopies of "CSI (Cartoon Sketch and Ink) handout (p. 127); pencils, black pens, and colorful markers; group journal supplies, marker (*Optional:* sheets of newsprint or butcher paper, tape)
			Option 2: Students watch a DVD version of "Out of Control" and discuss it. Or, choose to do both.	*Shocking and Scandalous Stories from the Bible* DVD, TV, and DVD player
Take 2: Feature Presentation	15 to 20 minutes	Dive into the Bible story and explore it together.	Small group and large group discussion	Photocopies of **Outtakes** (p. 128); medium or large yellow self-stick notes, markers, scissors *Optional:* Bibles
Take 3: Critics' Corner	15 to 20 minutes	Help your students grasp God's point of view and wrap things up with a fun team-building activity.	Discussion, game, and prayer	Photocopies of **Outtakes** (p. 128); group journal

Why Is This PG-13 Story in the Bible?

Herod's family had an "in" with the Roman government, which likely paid off with his appointment to govern Palestine. Also, they were Idumeans descended from Esau, the estranged brother of Jacob, the father of Israel. And he was far from easy to get along with. The slightest provocation triggered an "off with your head" reaction—literally. Herod even executed two of his wives and three of his sons because he perceived a threat. Obviously none of this made him popular with the Jews, so Herod constantly felt threatened.

Enter the Magi, or "wise men." Most likely they are from Persia or southern Arabia. Astrological studies cause them to spot a strange star, and their religious leaning enables them to realize it has spiritual significance. Their education may have given them some awareness of Jewish prophecies involving the "king of the Jews," so they follow the star to the Jewish capital, Jerusalem.

Is it possible the wise men are clueless about Herod's reputation? After all, *he* is the king of the Jews; why are they looking for anyone else? Herod is cordial but sneaky. "Find the child," he basically tells them, "and tell me where he is so I can worship him too" (see Matthew 2:8).

The star they have followed for such a long journey leads the wise men a few more miles to Bethlehem, where they find Jesus and worship him. When God uses a dream to warn them not to return to Herod, they hightail it out of town by a different route.

Herod is out-of-his mind furious. If there really is a baby king of the Jews out there, Herod wants him dead. He orders the slaughter of all boys in Bethlehem who are two years old and younger. God protects Jesus by telling Joseph in a dream to take his family and go to Egypt. Herod is too late—Jesus is kept safe. Herod's rage accomplishes nothing but needless suffering for innocent families.

Bethlehem was a smallish community; the number of baby boys in the target age bracket may have been only a couple of dozen. But Herod's action is nevertheless heinous—and completely in keeping with his character. From Herod's point of view, no violent rage is too high a price for looking out for number one.

> **Connecting with Community**
> Log on to www.shockingandscandalous.com to connect with other ministries:
> - Check out a sample video of other students in action.
> - Share with other leaders at the PG-13 forum about what's working in your ministry, what's not, or how you used *Shocking and Scandalous* this week.
> - Or ask for input about other aspects of middle school ministry.

9: Extreme Rampage

This story will help middle schoolers see the disaster that results when someone's feelings and actions are dominated by insecure, self-pleasing emotions.

Take It to Your Students

Here are some key points to put in front of your students with this lesson:
- This story fixes Jesus' birth at a specific time in human history—it's not mere legend.
- Emotions are God-given, but out-of-control rage is another thing.
- Extreme emotional reactions hurt innocent people. ✘

Extreme Rampage: The Lesson

Take 1: Preview (15 to 20 minutes)

Setup: This activity will set up the day's Bible story in a relational way as students create tyrant cartoons.

Props: Photocopies of CSI (Cartoon Sketch and Ink) handout (p. 127), 1 per student; pencils, black pens, and colorful markers; supplies for the journal option you've chosen

(*Optional:* sheets of newsprint or butcher paper, tape, *Shocking and Scandalous Stories from the Bible DVD*, TV, and DVD player)

QUIET ON THE SET

To launch the lesson:
- Welcome everyone to the group. Use first names or preferred nicknames and introduce visitors. After your students have had some time to socialize, pull them in and have them get comfortable.
- Go over your Rules of Engagement, if needed. (See the Rules of Engagement suggestions on p. 6 for more information.)
- Review the journaling component you've chosen for your group. (See Create a Group Journal on p. 10 for more information.)

ACTION

Read aloud the short story, "Anatomy of a Tyrant," from the CSI (Cartoon Sketch and Ink) handout. Then pass out the handout, one per student. Have each student pencil sketch a quick comic/cartoon likeness of the leader described in the story. Then instruct them to outline their drawings in black pen. Invite students to show their sketches to each other as they finish them.

PLAY BACK

Discuss the short story on the handout with your students, including the meaning of the word *tyrant*. Based on students' input, write a description of the tyrant's personality in the group journal. (Angry, hostile, bloodthirsty, uncontrolled, and so on.) Have your group decide on a name for the tyrant and describe what he might look like.

Now have students collaborate to draw one tyrant together. To do so, have them take turns drawing (or adding) single strokes to the image they're creating in the group journal until one original cartoon character emerges. Invite them to work together to fill it in with color and detail.

Use newsprint to cover an entire wall in your meeting area. Supply lots of colorful markers and invite students to sketch their tyrants directly on the wall, creating a collage of cartoons.

That's one angry, awful-looking tormentor!

DVD Option: Start off the group discussion that follows by first showing the "Out of Control" video on the *Shocking and Scandalous Stories from the Bible* DVD.

Use these questions to get a group discussion going:

- What's one thing people do that drives you crazy? Why does it bug you?
- What's something else that doesn't just annoy you—something that makes you *really* mad? Why does it upset you?
- How do you usually handle it when you feel really ticked off? When you feel so angry you're about to go over the edge?

Refer everyone back to the totally ticked-off tyrant they created, then ask:

- Describe what life might be like in a tyrant's kingdom. *(Miserable; awful; deadly; unbearable; all of the above)*
- What were the clues from today's story that helped you shape your cartoon character's image?
- What does ranting, raving, screaming, or bullying tell you about another person?

The stakes are high when leaders lose control. Let's investigate a tyrant's grim and brutal heart in today's **PG-13** feature, *Extreme Rampage*. ✗

9: Extreme Rampage

Take 2: Feature Presentation (15 to 20 minutes)

Setup: Your students will take a close look at the story of Herod ordering the murder of innocent babies and discuss out-of-control emotions.

Props: Photocopies of **Outtakes** (p. 128); medium or large yellow self-stick notes, markers, scissors
Optional: Bibles

QUIET ON THE SET

Pass out copies of **Outtakes**, one per student. *Optional:* Have students grab their own Bibles.

ACTION

Use **Outtakes** to introduce and teach the Bible story. First, briefly introduce the **Cast** and make sure your students know who's who. Next, use **Movie Trailer** to cover the highlights of the Bible background and story. Then read the Bible story (Matthew 2:1-15) out loud from **Outtakes** or have a volunteer read it. If you prefer, ask students to read the passages from their own Bibles.

PLAY BACK

Divide your group into two or more small teams with an adult or older teen leader for each discussion group. Have half of the groups examine the story from Herod's point of view (Team Talk 1) and have the remaining groups look into things from the wise men's perspective (Team Talk 2). Remind group leaders to be ready to enhance discussion with insights from **Why Is This PG-13 Story In the Bible?** (p. 118).

Give each group yellow paper, scissors, and markers. As they talk about the questions below, have students write on yellow self-stick notes the motivations that they see in the story characters. Some students might enjoy sketching picture answers to the questions. At the end of their discussion, each group can arrange their sticky notes on a window or wall to resemble an explosive star. Remind students that stars are balls of gas, not simply five points, so they can be creative in the arrangement.

The wise men and Herod had extremely different mind-sets. Let's do a mind sweep and discover what they were.

Team Talk 1: Get into Herod's head.

- If you could describe Herod in just three words, what would they be? Why?
- In your opinion, what's Herod's number one priority? *(To be the only king.)*
- How does Herod show his anxiety? *(Gathers people for information; arranges a secret meeting)*
- How does Herod try to fool the wise men? *(Pretends to want to worship Jesus.)*
- When Herod loses control, what happens? *(He orders the slaughter of babies. Innocent people get hurt.)*

Team Talk 2: Get into the wise men's heads.

- Are the wise men looking for anything for themselves? Explain.
- In your opinion, what's the wise men's number one priority in this story? *(To find Jesus and worship him.)*
- What's the high point of this story for the wise men? *(Finding Jesus.)*
- The wise men disobey the king's direct order and sneak out of town. Was it wrong for them to do so? Make your case.
- How do the wise men show what's really in their hearts? *(They actively seek; they give gifts generously; they listen to God.)*

Bring the discussion teams back together. Arrange the teams' stars so the rays interlock and combine to make one big fiery ball taped to the wall. Briefly review discussion results by reading what's written on the self-stick note stars.

Continue your discussion as a large group by asking questions like:

- In what ways are the wise men the opposite of Herod? *(They wanted to worship Jesus; Herod wanted to eliminate Jesus.)*
- What emotions get out of control for Herod to the point that he will kill babies? *(Worry, fear, threat, rage)*
- Why do you think this story about slaughtering babies is in the Bible?

Herod is on edge trying to protect his kingship. He loses it when foreigners show up looking for someone *born* to be king, not someone *appointed* to be king by the Roman government. His hysterical rage devastates innocent families.

9: Extreme Rampage

Ask the group questions like:
- Where in the story could Herod have made other choices? Be specific.
- How could the story have been different if Herod controlled his emotions?
- How do you think the Key Verse (Proverbs 29:11) illustrates this story?

Emotions are not wrong. God made us emotional beings. But we have to be careful not to allow emotions to think for us. Herod's intense response blinded him, and with it came the death of innocent baby boys.

Take 3: Critics' Corner (15 to 20 minutes)

Setup: Reinforce the points you want your students to take away from today's lesson.
Props: Group journal with entries from Take 1; **Outtakes** (p. 128)

QUIET ON THE SET

Grab the group journal and draw the group's attention to the tyrant "CSI" cartoon character drawn earlier.

ACTION

Consider the POV

Together, compare King Herod to the cartoon character in the group journal and discuss any similarities between the two. Then write the words, "aka (also known as) King Herod" under the cartoon image.

Draw students' attention to the **POV** on the **Outtakes** handout: *Emotional reactions cast God's wisdom aside and hurt innocent people.*

Life can be tough. It's tougher with an angry heart.

> Just a reminder that the **bold** text in these lessons are suggestions for what you can say as you teach. Remember that this isn't a script; always feel free to take our ideas and put them in your own words.

Discuss the powerful feeling of anger with your group. Ask:
- What does angry behavior—shouting, hitting, hurting, cursing—communicate to others? *(I'm more wrapped up with "me" than "we.")*

- Is there a trusted someone you can turn to when your feelings get the better of you? How does sharing with others help you keep your cool?
- **How can feelings be expressed positively?** *(Describe your feelings in words to help others understand why you're upset.)*

Understand God's Truth

Angry emotional outbursts affect others in painful ways. When we ignore God's wisdom and act upon feelings alone, the result is stress, hurt, despair, and separation.

Ask the group:

- **What have we learned from today's story?** *(Herod was furious that the wise men outsmarted him and sought his revenge on innocent children.)*
- **What was Herod's downfall?** *(His obsessive attempt to kill Jesus; his uncontrollable rage and lack of self-control)*

Today's Bible verse in Proverbs 29:11 teaches, "A fool gives full vent to his anger, but a wise man keeps himself under control." This is a life-lesson that an angry and obsessed Herod never bothered to master.

Teamwork

Sometimes it can be tough to control our own anger—but our friends can help us do it. Let's be there for each other this week as we try to honor God in the way we deal with our feelings.

PLAY BACK

Wrap up the meeting with an anger-themed team-building game. Then close in prayer.

ICE (In Case of Emergency)

Needed: no supplies needed
Goal: Avoid becoming the next angry "It."

How to Play:

Ask a volunteer to be "It." Divide your group in half and form two game circles, an inner and an outer ring. Outer ring players should stand directly

9: Extreme Rampage

behind inner ring players. "It" will take his or her position in the center.

Play begins when "It" suddenly erupts in anger, demonstrated by slow-to-fast-to-furious clapping. The inner ring picks up the cue and starts clapping as well. When the clapping becomes frenzied, "It" shouts "Ice!" and the outer ring panics! Players run off in all directions to the edges of the playing area. After awhile, "It" decides to "cool it" and abruptly stops clapping. The inner ring takes the cue and does the same. "It" and the outer ring must now compete to find an open space behind an inner ring player. The extra player who cannot find a space becomes the new angry "It." Switch inner and outer ring positions once during play.

> For large groups, set rings in motion in opposite directions. After the "panic," have inner and outer ring players pair up, lock arms, and walk together clockwise. For a small group, "It" can clap alone while others scatter. When the clapping stops, the last one back to the circle or a line becomes the new "It."

(If your group does not divide evenly, widen the circle and assign one, two, or three "angry Its." "Angry Its" will need to establish secret clues [such as eye winks, nose twitch, foot taps] for when to begin and end clapping.)

After the game, say: **Chill, man! Anger spreads quickly and is hard to contain once it explodes. In case of an anger emergency, keep your cool to see God's big picture. Remember, extreme emotional reactions hurt innocent people.**

Close with Prayer

Ask your group to look again at **Outtakes** and repeat today's **Key Verse**: "A fool gives full vent to his anger, but a wise man keeps himself under control" (Proverbs 29:11). Then point out this week's *Verse-ability: Losing control just makes me look foolish.* Encourage your students to keep God's truth front and center in their lives this week. If time permits, jot the verse in the group journal and have everyone initial it.

> If you sense some of your students are struggling with anger toward God, let them know you're available to talk privately.

Before prayers, take a "pulse check" of your group. Say: **Extreme situations present even greater opportunities for God to shine through. Do you know of one, two, or more of your friends who may be angry with God for a past abuse** or wrong? Without sharing private details, ask the group to cup their hands, raise them over their heads, and silently offer the hurts of their friends—or their own hurts—up to God. Have prayers zero in on these intense emotions and ask God's Spirit to break their hold. After prayer, have everyone "throw" the hurts away. ✘

Verse-atility: *Losing control just makes me look foolish.*

CSI (Cartoon Sketch and Ink)

Anatomy of a Tyrant
A SHORT, SHORT STORY...

Thick storm clouds gathered. The leader's words, bitter and poisonous, came slowly.

Upon hearing the decree, the commander of the north armies fell to his knees. "But... my lord... we cannot take the lives of children!"

The leader's crimson cape twisted in the arid breeze. His trembling sword pointed to the heavens. His sudden hysterical scream spoke not of sanity but of madness.

"No one will take my kingdom! Kill them, kill them all!"

Instructions: Use your imagination and sketch a cartoon character based on the leader in today's story in the box below. Outline the final likeness in pen.

Permission is granted by Standard Publishing to reproduce this handout for ministry purposes only (not for resale).

Outtakes

CAST

Magi: "wise men" and "scholars," probably astrologers or scholars, from lands east of Israel
Herod: appointed by the Roman government to rule the Jews
Joseph: husband of Mary, the mother of Jesus

MOVIE TRAILER

- Wise men come to Jerusalem looking for the new king of the Jews.
- Herod wants to get rid of the new king—Jesus—and tries to get the wise men to help him.
- The wise men find Jesus, then outsmart Herod and avoid seeing him again.
- Herod discovers the wise men have gotten away and decides to kill all the baby boys in Bethlehem to make sure Jesus is dead.
- An angel warns Joseph to take Mary and Jesus away to Egypt.

Verse-atility: Losing control just makes me look foolish.

POV: Emotional reactions cast God's wisdom aside and hurt innocent people.
Key Verse: A fool gives full vent to his anger, but a wise man keeps himself under control (Proverbs 29:11).

EXTREME RAMPAGE

Mathew 2:1-16 *(The Message) (We've added a few of our own comments in **bold** below.)*

After Jesus was born in Bethlehem village, Judah territory—this was during Herod's kingship—a band of scholars **[you know them as the wise men]** arrived in Jerusalem from the East. They asked around, "Where can we find and pay homage to the newborn King of the Jews? We observed a star in the eastern sky that signaled his birth. We're on pilgrimage to worship him."

When word of their inquiry got to Herod, he was terrified—and not Herod alone, but most of Jerusalem as well. Herod lost no time. He gathered all the high priests and religion scholars in the city together and asked, "Where is the Messiah supposed to be born?"

They told him, "Bethlehem, Judah territory. The prophet Micah wrote it plainly:
It's you, Bethlehem, in Judah's land, no longer bringing up the rear. From you will come the leader who will shepherd-rule my people, my Israel."

Herod then arranged a secret meeting with the scholars from the East. Pretending to be as devout as they were, he got them to tell him exactly when the birth-announcement star appeared. Then he told them the prophecy about Bethlehem, and said, "Go find this child. Leave no stone unturned. As soon as you find him, send word and I'll join you at once in your worship." **[Liar, liar!]**

Instructed by the king, they set off. Then the star appeared again, the same star they had seen in the eastern skies. It led them on until it hovered over the place of the child. They could hardly contain themselves: They were in the right place! They had arrived at the right time!

They entered the house and saw the child in the arms of Mary, his mother. Overcome, they kneeled and worshiped him. Then they opened their luggage and presented gifts: gold, frankincense, myrrh.

In a dream, they were warned not to report back to Herod. So they worked out another route, left the territory without being seen, and returned to their own country.

After the scholars were gone, God's angel showed up again in Joseph's dream and commanded, "Get up. Take the child and his mother and flee to Egypt. Stay until further notice. Herod is on the hunt for this child, and wants to kill him."

Joseph obeyed. He got up, took the child and his mother under cover of darkness. They were out of town and well on their way by daylight. They lived in Egypt until Herod's death. This Egyptian exile fulfilled what Hosea had preached: "I called my son out of Egypt."

Herod, when he realized that the scholars had tricked him, flew into a rage **[out-of-his-mind crazy]**. He commanded the murder of every little boy two years old and under who lived in Bethlehem and its surrounding hills. **[Let's call him Herod, The Bloodthirsty.]**

Permission is granted by Standard Publishing to reproduce this **Outtakes** handout for ministry purposes only (not for resale).

10 Resident Evil

Director's Commentary

NOW SHOWING: *Resident Evil*

FROM THE BIBLE: Satan tempts Jesus to sell out (Matthew 4:1-11).

RATED PG-13 FOR: the self-serving, seductive, feel-good nature of temptation; attempted demonic possession

POV: Don't let temptation twist who you are.

KEY VERSE: "May integrity and uprightness protect me, because my hope is in you" (Psalm 25:21).

The Lesson	Time	What you'll do ...	How you'll do it ...	What you'll need ...
Take 1: Preview	15 to 20 minutes	Start off your lesson by introducing the theme with a relational, creative activity.	Option 1: Students act out "Survival of the Fittest 101" drama and discuss it.	4 copies of "Survival of the Fittest 101" (pp. 139, 140); group journal supplies, marker (*Optional:* items from your prop box, hats, sunglasses, digital camera, an empty water bottle, backpacks, notebook, pen, map, cell phone, real or fake snacks, walking sticks, movie snacks)
			Option 2: Students watch a DVD version of "Survival of the Fittest 101" and discuss it. Or, choose to do both.	*Shocking and Scandalous Stories from the Bible* DVD, TV, and DVD player; group journal supplies
Take 2: Feature Presentation	15 to 20 minutes	Dive into the Bible story and explore it together.	Small group and large group discussion	Photocopies of **Outtakes** (p. 141); beige or brown paper, markers, scissors, tape *Optional:* Bibles
Take 3: Critics' Corner	15 to 20 minutes	Help your students grasp God's point of view and wrap things up with a fun team-building activity.	Discussion, game, and prayer	Photocopies of **Outtakes** (p. 141); group journal, marker; table tennis balls (1 per pair), coffee mugs (1 per player) (*Optional:* 2 clear drinking glasses, water, mineral oil, 2 saltine crackers, spoon)

Why Is This PG-13 Story in the Bible?

Talk about ups and downs. The last part of Matthew 3 tells the story of Jesus being baptized. Heaven opened and the Spirit of God descended on him. He heard God the Father say, "This is my Son, whom I love" (3:17). It doesn't get higher than that. Then, that same Spirit led Jesus into the desert. Why? To be tempted by the devil. It doesn't get lower than that.

Temptation doesn't hit Jesus in the face immediately. First Jesus spends forty days and nights all alone . . . with no food. Jesus is at his most vulnerable point, and that's when the devil shows up. Talk about strategic timing! Keep in mind it was no surprise; the Spirit takes Jesus to the desert for a purpose. But after forty days of hunger, it's easy to imagine how perspectives could change. That's what makes it a genuine temptation.

> **Connecting with Community**
> Log on to www.shockingandscandalous.com to connect with other ministries:
> - Check out a sample video of other students in action.
> - Share with other leaders at the PG-13 forum about what's working in your ministry, what's not, or how you used *Shocking and Scandalous* this week.
> - Or ask for input about other aspects of middle school ministry.

The devil tempts Jesus in three ways. Turning stones into bread would satisfy his immediate physical need. Jumping off the temple and letting angels catch him would be a sensational, attention-getting stunt. And a simple act of worshiping Satan would give Jesus possession of the whole world. The point of all three temptations is to entice Jesus to turn his back on the job he came to earth to do. Jesus' mission to be the Savior of the world would destroy Satan's power; clearly the devil has a vested interest in making Jesus misuse his authority as the Son of God. If Jesus gives in to temptation, the devil wins.

Unquestionably, Jesus is hungry and weak, a reminder of his humanity. Both Jesus and Satan know what the Scriptures say. The difference is that Satan twists God's own words to justify giving in to temptation, and Jesus stands on God's words as the grounds for resisting temptation. He doesn't give in to doubt or weakness or imagining what could be. Jesus knows he is God's Son, and even this suffering is part of what God wants him to go through in order to be the Savior of the world. He knows his identity and that he belongs to God, and passing this test proves he is qualified to be our Savior.

10: Resident Evil

This Bible story will help your students see there is an alternative to giving in to temptation. Because Jesus did it, we can do it.

Take It to Your Students

Here are some key points to put in front of your students with this lesson:
- Temptation happens to everyone, even Jesus.
- When you feel tempted, consider how it will change you.
- Remember, you belong to God first. ✘

Resident Evil: The Lesson

Take 1: Preview (15 to 20 minutes)

Setup: This activity will set up the day's Bible story in a relational way as students watch one person panic when tempted to abandon his friends.

Set design: Create a relaxed atmosphere for *Preview*. Ask students to sit on the floor in a circle on pillows, seat cushions, or colorful mats. The drama will be performed in the middle. Movie snacks like popcorn can add to the mood.

Makeup and effects: For today's drama use your one-size-fits-all prop box.

Props: Supplies for the journal option you've chosen, markers; 4 copies of "Survival of the Fittest 101" (pp. 139, 140) or the *Shocking and Scandalous Stories from the Bible DVD* and a TV with DVD player
(*Optional:* items from your prop box, hats, sunglasses, digital camera, an empty water bottle, backpacks, notebook, pen, map, cell phone, plastic snacks, walking sticks, movie snacks for your audience)

QUIET ON THE SET

To launch the lesson:
- Welcome everyone to the group. Use first names or preferred nicknames and introduce visitors. After your students have had some time to socialize, pull them in and have them get comfortable.
- Briefly go over your Rules of Engagement, if needed. (See the Rules of Engagement suggestions on p. 6 for more information.)

- Review the journaling component you've chosen for your group. (See Create a Group Journal on p. 10 for more information.)

ACTION

Either have students perform the "Survival of the Fittest 101" skit, watch "Survival of the Fittest 101" on the *Shocking and Scandalous Stories from the Bible DVD*, or do both. If you choose to have students perform the skit live, give copies of "Survival of the Fittest 101" (pp. 139, 140) to your student actors and have them prep by reading through their parts a time or two. Also, invite the actors to rummage through the prop box for items to enhance their performance.

> If you want, make a video of your students' live performance of "Survival of the Fittest 101." Play it back later, perhaps for the entire church.

PLAY BACK

Use the discussion ideas below to reflect on "Survival of the Fittest 101" with your group. Don't edit your students' responses—allow them to discuss freely.

Survivalists know that there are risk factors when trekking in the wilderness. Based on today's skit, let's make a list of how we might be tempted to lose our heads in a desperate situation.

Ask a volunteer to print today's date and "Risk Factors for Wilderness Survival" on the top of the journal page. Risk factors could include thirst, hunger, heat stress, broken bones, getting lost, flash floods, cold nights, severe storms, snakebites, wild animals, injuries, and more.

Use the questions below to discuss Caleb's behavior in the skit or video. Have a volunteer record the group's thoughts and impressions in the group journal. Give every student the opportunity to comment or to journal, even if it is just to initial in agreement with posted entries.

Now, let's revisit Caleb in today's drama.

Use these questions to get a group discussion going:

- Where would Caleb register on a stress meter? Low, medium, or high? Explain.
- What are the "risk factors" in Caleb's behavior?
- How do they escalate tension within the group?
- Do you think you would have been tempted to make the same choice as Caleb? Why or why not?

10: Resident Evil

- How would you score on a "stress test" in the wilderness?
- What do you think the rest of the group should do now?

When stress builds, who we are and what we stand for can be tested.

Up next: Enter a desert-hot world where the super naturals collide. Meet a hell-raiser and a Savior. The Savior submits to punishing temptation but never, ever, relinquishes his identity. *Resident Evil,* straight ahead. ✘

Take 2: Feature Presentation (15 to 20 minutes)

Setup: Your students will take a close look at the story of Jesus' temptation and discuss hanging on to our identity in Christ.

Props: Photocopies of **Outtakes** (p. 141); beige or brown paper, markers, scissors, tape

Optional: Bibles

QUIET ON THE SET

Pass out copies of **Outtakes,** one per student.
Optional: Have students grab their own Bibles.

ACTION

Use **Outtakes** to introduce and teach the Bible story. First, briefly introduce the **Cast** and make sure your students know who's who. Next, use **Movie Trailer** to cover the highlights of the Bible background and story.

> Your students might get tripped up here because Jesus was fully God and fully human. They may think his divinity somehow made it super easy for Jesus to turn Satan down. If needed, take a moment to explore this question further with your group, helping them see that Jesus fully experienced the depth of human temptation (see Hebrews 2:17, 18; 4:15, 16).

Then read the Bible story (Matthew 4:1-11) out loud from **Outtakes** or have a volunteer read it. If you prefer, ask students to read the passage aloud from their own Bibles.

PLAY BACK

Divide your group into two or more small teams for discussion with an adult or older teen leader for each group. Assign half of the groups to explore Jesus' role in this story (Team Talk 1) and the remaining groups to look at Satan's role

(Team Talk 2). Remind group leaders to be ready to enhance discussion with insights from **Why Is This PG-13 Story in the Bible?** (p. 130).

Give each student a piece of paper, a marker, and scissors. Before discussion begins, ask students to scrunch up their papers, smooth them open, and step on them. Then have them cut their papers into the shape of something in the desert (a rock, cactus, scrubby bushes) and fray the edges.

Have students discuss the questions in their teams and record their answers by writing key phrases on the desert shapes they've cut.

Let's head out to the wilderness to witness a diabolical test.

Team Talk 1: Get into the head of Jesus.

- In your opinion, what was at the heart of the three tests Jesus faced? *(Essentially, the devil wanted Jesus to bring attention to himself, rather than his Father and the work he had to do.)*
- What methods did Jesus use to pass the test? *(Remembered who he is; used God's words)*
- Why would Jesus think it's important to pass this big test? *(If Jesus failed this test, he would not be the Savior.)*
- What do you think motivated Jesus to resist temptation? What motivates you?

> Just a reminder that we've included examples of possible student answers to some of the discussion questions in these lessons. You'll see them in *italics*. If your students get stuck on a question, share one of the sample answers to help them get their discussion started.

Team Talk 2: Get into the head of Satan.

- What did the devil try to get Jesus to do? Why? *(Essentially, the devil wanted Jesus to bring attention to himself, rather than his Father and the work he had to do.)*
- What would Satan stand to gain if Jesus gave in to temptation? What did he have to lose if Jesus stood firm? *(If Jesus gave in, he couldn't be the Savior and break Satan's power.)*
- What super-sneaky methods did the devil try? *(Approached Jesus at his lowest point; twisted God's words; used multiple temptations)*
- What super-sneaky methods does the devil try to use with you?

Bring the discussion teams back together. Have students tape their desert shapes on the blank wall to create a desert scene, then briefly review what they wrote.

10: Resident Evil

Continue your discussion as a large group by asking questions like:

- **Jesus was fully human—just like we are. What gave him the ability to resist temptation?**
- **What was at the heart of what the devil tried to do?**
- **Who came out on top?**
- **Why do you think this story is in the Bible?** *(This is an opportunity to remind students of the Key Verse: "May integrity and uprightness protect me, because my hope is in you" [Psalm 25:21].)*

God sent Jesus into the world with a mission—to become our Savior. If Satan's temptation had distracted Jesus, where would we be? Although weakened, Jesus remained rock-solid in his identity.

Let's look again at the devil's brazen attack in this story.

Ask the group questions like:

- **What if Jesus had decided to eat some bread? What would that have changed?**
- **How well does the devil know those things that appeal and tempt you?**
- **What can we learn from how Jesus responded to temptation?**

Jesus knew who he was. He was his Father's Son. Jesus could not separate himself from the truth of Scripture. We belong to the Father too. Don't allow temptation to twist who you are. Know your Bible. Know you belong to God. ✘

Take 3: Critics' Corner (15 to 20 minutes)

Setup: Reinforce the points you want your students to take away from today's lesson.

Props: Group journal with entries from Take 1; **Outtakes** (p. 141); table tennis balls, 1 per pair; coffee mugs, 1 per player
(*Optional:* 2 clear drinking glasses, water, mineral oil, 2 saltine crackers, spoon)

QUIET ON THE SET

Grab the group journal and ask students to gather to review their "Survival of the Fittest 101" entries from Take 1.

ACTION

Consider the POV

Ask the group:

- **How did Jesus handle stress-relieving temptation?** *(Jesus faced temptation but did not give in to it. He relied on his Father for help.)*

Review students' suggested endings for the skit recorded in the group journal (from the discussion question "What do you think the rest of the group should do now?"). After each entry is read, ask your students to give a thumbs up or down on whether the entry reflects today's **POV**. If your students have new insights, write them down now.

Draw students' attention to the POV on the **Outtakes** handout: *Don't let temptation twist who you are.* Then ask the group:

- **What do you see as the top three temptations students your age face?**
- **How could giving in to these temptation twist the real you and affect your choices?**

Optional: To demonstrate remaining strong in Christ to your group, perform this simple experiment. Fill two glasses half full, one with water, the other with mineral oil. Submerge a saltine cracker into each glass. Proceed with the discussion—you'll come back to this experiment later.

Understand God's Truth

Jesus remained true to himself. By passing Satan's test, he proved himself qualified to be the Savior.

Ask the group:

- **What have we learned from today's story?** *(When Jesus was at his weakest point, Satan attacked his identity.)*
- **As Christians, we believe in impossible and unseen things—including our belief in Satan's existence and his very real efforts to derail us. Reflect on Satan's temptations and how they influence your actions. How do you feel when you think about Satan's efforts to get your faith off-track? How do you want to respond?** *(I won't allow little things or tough things to come along and define me.)*

Satan did his evil-best to make Jesus doubt himself. But Jesus relied on his Father's holy Word and became the standard by which we now live.

Teamwork

Just as Jesus relied heavily on his Father to get him through tempting times, we can rely on him and each other to resist temptation this week.

PLAY BACK

Wrap up the meeting with a team-building game that's full of temptation. Then close in prayer.

Mug Shot

Needed: table tennis balls, coffee mugs
Goal: Catch table tennis balls in coffee mugs.

> **Verse-atility:** *God, keep me real and true; I depend on you.*

How to Play:

This game requires uncarpeted floor space for maximum fun on the bounce. Have students pair up. Give each player a coffee mug and one table tennis ball per pair. Drop the balls into mugs. The object of the game is for Player 1 to blow the ball out of his or her mug (not easy!) while Player 2 tries to catch it in flight or on a bounce (not easy either!). The temptation is to use hands. For instance, Player 2 will be tempted to use a free hand to keep the ball from bouncing out of the mug. Sorry, no hands allowed! Have pairs keep trying to pass their ball back and forth in this weird way.

Or try another version of the game: Players gently swing the ball out of the mug and have partners catch it with their mug. Players must cooperate to complete ten mug-catches. Balls must stay in mugs—no bouncing out—to score points. Again, no hands.

After the game, say: **Great job! Resisting temptation is the hard part, isn't it? Giving in to it, much easier.**

Have players catch their breath. If you started the *optional* experiment earlier, say: **Let's get back to our little experiment I set up earlier.**

Draw the group's attention back to the two glasses of liquid. **Both glasses look the same from the outside.**

Take the spoon and lift the crackers. One cracker (in the mineral oil) will retain its shape; the other (in water) will simply fall apart.

Temptation is a force—one that works to dissolve your identity in Christ. Don't allow it to have power in your life.

Close with Prayer

Ask your group to look again at **Outtakes** and repeat today's **Key Verse:** "May integrity and uprightness protect me, because my hope is in you" (Psalm 25:21). Then point out this week's *Verse-atility: God, keep me real and true; I depend on you.* If time permits, jot the verse in the group journal and have everyone initial it.

Invite students to share prayer requests, especially about their efforts to resist temptation, and then close in prayer.

> If you think your students can handle it maturely (without goofing off or breaking confidentiality), have them form pairs for this prayer time. Boys should pray with boys and girls should pray with girls. Challenge them to share with each other one area of temptation they're dealing with; prompt them to pray for each other's requests.

Survival of the Fittest 101

Characters:
NARRATOR
CALEB and TROY: two middle school guys in the school's science club
SUSAN and TIFFANY: two middle school girls in the school's science club
Scene: A state park forested area or wilderness-like area. The four friends are doing an observation project for the science club.
Prop Suggestions: Select any props or costumes you want from the prop box. Also, if you want, use hats, sunglasses, digital camera, an empty water bottle, backpacks, notebook, pen, map, cell phone, plastic snacks, and walking sticks (or just pretend!).

SCRIPT

(All four students are walking together in the forest of a state park or wilderness area. They are secluded from society, but they're looking around, excited, ready to have fun.)

CALEB:
(walks to a stopping point) **Alright. Our job is to take pictures of all the snakes we can find out here.**

SUSAN:
(adjusting her digital camera; Susan brings this line in an intentionally cheesy, over-the-top way) **Slithers, sliders, and sidewinders, huh? Sounds snake-tastic!!**

CALEB:
We'll take pictures of the snakes . . .

TIFFANY:
. . . From a safe distance!

CALEB:
. . . and then, we'll record all their information. Like their behavior, their environment—everything.

TROY:
I'm on it.

(Caleb picks ups his pack and swings it over his shoulder. The group continues on, ready to get to work. Walk "off stage.")

TIME LAPSE. IT IS MUCH LATER IN THE DAY. NIGHTFALL IS NEARING . . .

TIFFANY:
I'm so hungry. Let's take a break.

(The group comes to a halt, ready to take a break, setting backpacks down.)

CALEB:
(looking very tired) **Troy, food and water. Throw me something from your pack.**

(Troy fumbles through his pack. He pull outs an empty water bottle and has an empty look on his face . . .)

TROY:
Uh oh . . .

CALEB:
(clearly irritated, glaring in annoyance at Troy) **Dude**, it was your responsibility this morning to get food and water from the cooler before we left camp.

TROY:
I thought that was Susan's job. I have the compass and bug spray.

TIFFANY:
Are you telling me we're stuck in the middle of the forest with no water?! Oh yeah, and I'm still hungry.

SUSAN:
(*searches through her pack*) I have the rain gear. No water. No food. Who has the protein bars?

TROY:
Not me. I have the compass and bug spray.

CALEB:
(*Starting to get mean; the bully in him is coming out*) We already know what you have, Troy. And it *isn't* a brain.

SUSAN:
Hey, Caleb, chill! Ripping on Troy isn't going to help anything.

CALEB:
(*starting to panic*) Seriously, though, we've been out here all day. In about two hours we'll be dehydrated. People *die* without water, Susan!

SUSAN:
(*holds up map for Caleb to see*) Let's not panic. I have the map. We'll figure something out. We're OK!

CALEB:
(*desperately searches for his cell phone, finds it, and looks at it, then shakes his head in disappointment*) Just what I thought! No connection.

TROY:
Caleb, enough.

CALEB:
(*Now completely turning on Troy*) This is all your fault. (*raising his voice even further*) All YOUR FAULT!

TIFFANY:
Wow. This is *not* the Caleb I know.

SUSAN:
Yeah, Caleb, that's *not* fair. We all should have checked our packs before we left. And besides, when it gets dark our parents will come looking for us.

CALEB:
(*steps forward and rips the map from Susan's hands*) I . . . I can't wait for this. . . . . I've got the map—I've got a phone.

SUSAN:
Hey!

CALEB:
I'm gonna find my own way back to camp.

TIFFANY:
(*in disbelief*) You can't just *leave* us!

CALEB:
(*Caleb walks on, fully determined to leave his friends. He turns back, one time, to shout at them . . .*) Watch me!

(*The three remaining friends look at each other, unsure what to do next.*)

(*Skit ends; actors rejoin group.*)

Permission is granted by Standard Publishing to reproduce this "Survival of the Fittest 101" script for ministry purposes only (not for resale).

Outtakes

CAST
Jesus: facing a test of his true identity as the Son of God
Satan: tries to make Jesus fail the test

MOVIE TRAILER
- After Jesus is baptized by John, the Holy Spirit takes him into the wilderness.
- After forty days of fasting, the devil comes to him to tempt him.
- The devil tempts Jesus three times, but Jesus answers every time by quoting Scripture.
- Finally the devil gives up and leaves. Angels take care of Jesus.

Verse-atility: God, keep me real and true; I depend on you.

POV: Don't let temptation twist who you are.
Key Verse: May integrity and uprightness protect me, because my hope is in you (Psalm 25:21).

RESIDENT EVIL

Mathew 4:1-11 *(The Message)*
*(We've added a few of our own comments **in bold** below.)*

Next Jesus was taken into the wild by the Spirit for the Test. The Devil was ready to give it. **[Evil brings it on!]** Jesus prepared for the Test by fasting forty days and forty nights. That left him, of course, in a state of extreme hunger, which the Devil took advantage of in the first test: "Since you are God's Son, speak the word that will turn these stones into loaves of bread." **[When you are *that* hungry, quite tempting . . .]**

Jesus answered by quoting Deuteronomy: "It takes more than bread to stay alive. It takes a steady stream of words from God's mouth."

For the second test the Devil took him to the Holy City. He sat him on top of the Temple and said, "Since you are God's Son, jump." The Devil goaded him by quoting Psalm 91: "He has placed you in the care of angels. They will catch you so that you won't so much as stub your toe on a stone."

Jesus countered with another citation from Deuteronomy: "Don't you dare test the Lord your God."

For the third test, the Devil took him to the peak of a huge mountain. He gestured expansively, pointing out all the earth's kingdoms, how glorious they all were. Then he said, "They're yours—lock, stock, and barrel. Just go down on your knees and worship me, and they're yours."

Jesus' refusal was curt: "Beat it, Satan!" **[No messin' with the Savior!]** He backed his rebuke with a third quotation from Deuteronomy: "Worship the Lord your God, and only him. Serve him with absolute single-heartedness."

The Test was over. The Devil left. And in his place, angels! Angels came and took care of Jesus' needs. **[R(est) & R(elaxation) for Jesus.]**

*Permission is granted by Standard Publishing to reproduce this **Outtakes** handout for ministry purposes only (not for resale).*

11 Dirty Dancing

Director's Commentary

NOW SHOWING: *Dirty Dancing*
FROM THE BIBLE: Salome dances for King Herod (Mark 6:17-29).
RATED PG-13 FOR: sensuality involving a teen, partying, and gruesome execution
POV: Be careful what you allow into your heart; influences turn into actions with final consequences.
KEY VERSE: "Above all else, guard your heart, for it is the wellspring of life" (Proverbs 4:23).

The Lesson	Time	What you'll do . . .	How you'll do it . . .	What you'll need . . .
Take 1: Preview	15 to 20 minutes	Start off your lesson by introducing the theme with a relational, creative activity.	Option 1: Students act out "A Lousy Feeling" drama and discuss it.	5 to 9 copies of "A Lousy Feeling" (pp. 151, 152); group journal supplies, markers (*Optional:* items from your prop box, a cell phone, popcorn, TV, iPod with speakers, movie snacks for your audience)
			Option 2: Students watch a DVD version of "A Lousy Feeling" and discuss it. Or, choose to do both.	*Shocking and Scandalous Stories from the Bible DVD*, TV and DVD player; markers, group journal supplies
Take 2: Feature Presentation	15 to 20 minutes	Dive into the Bible story and explore it together.	Small group and large group discussion	Photocopies of **Outtakes** (p. 153); 4 flip charts (or 4 large pieces of paper and tape), markers or pens *Optional:* Bibles
Take 3: Critics' Corner	15 to 20 minutes	Help your students grasp God's point of view and wrap things up with a fun team-building activity.	Discussion, game, and prayer	Photocopies of **Outtakes** (p. 153); group journal; individual snack-size M&M or Skittle candy bags (about 2 bags per student), 2 or more large bowls

11: Dirty Dancing

Why Is This PG-13 Story in the Bible?

Herod Antipas, the Roman-appointed Jewish ruler of Galilee, respects and fears John the Baptist, the outspoken prophet who calls for repentance. But repentance is not on Herod's agenda—it would get in the way of his seduction of Herodias, his brother's wife. Characteristically, John calls things the way they are: Herod and Herodias are committing adultery. Because John calls them out, Herodias wants John dead—so she bides her time, watchful for an opportunity.

When Herod's birthday arrives, he throws himself a huge, lewd party. Alcohol likely flows until Herod and his guests are long past caring about much of anything. The banquet hall is full of people whom Herod wants to impress. His stepdaughter—the Jewish historian Josephus tells us the girl's name was Salome—becomes the main entertainment with a dance. Young and no doubt dressed seductively, she is something a room full of men in a drunken orgy would covet.

Imagine Herod's chest swelling when he sees his guests enjoying the entertainment. Generosity washes over him, and Herod publicly promises to give Salome anything she wants—"up to half my kingdom." In his euphoric state, he does not imagine she will ask for the head of John the Baptist. But that's what Salome asks for because that's what Herodias wants.

> **Connecting with Community**
> Log on to www.shockingandscandalous.com to connect with other ministries:
> - Check out a sample video of other students in action.
> - Share with other leaders at the PG-13 forum about what's working in your ministry, what's not, or how you used *Shocking and Scandalous* this week.
> - Or ask for input about other aspects of middle school ministry.

What will he look like in front of his guests if he backtracks now? Herod chooses to protect his dignity and orders the death of John. This isn't a tidy execution—one with drugs pumped into John's veins to make sure he doesn't suffer. Prisoners have no rights, not even the right to be treated humanely. In the dismal Machaerus castle, the prison Herod used as a fortress on the Dead Sea, John's head is crudely severed from his body. An unnamed servant has the ghastly task of carrying John's head on a platter and presenting it to Salome. She then presents it to her mother, Herodias.

Herod is a lustful man who stole his brother's wife and used his stepdaughter for the pleasure of others. He did things he knew were wrong because others pressured him—and that trapped him in a dangerous game where he thinks he has no choice. This Bible story will help students understand the impact behind the decisions and choices they make every day.

Take It to Your Students

Here are some key points to put in front of your students with this lesson:
- Question your actions when you feel trapped.
- Consider carefully whether you have no choice in such situations.
- Look closely at what's influencing your choices and the consequences that could result. ✘

Dirty Dancing: The Lesson

Take 1: Preview (15 to 20 minutes)

Setup: This activity will set up the day's Bible story in a relational way as students explore how one teen responds when an unplanned party breaks out in her living room.

Set design: Create a relaxed atmosphere for *Preview*. Have students sit on the floor in a large circle on pillows, cushions, or rugs. The activity can be performed in the center. Popcorn or other movie snacks can also help set the mood.

Makeup and effects: Have students use your one-size-fits-all prop box.

Props: Supplies for the journal option you've chosen, markers; 5 to 9 copies of "A Lousy Feeling" (pp. 151, 152) or the *Shocking and Scandalous Stories from the Bible DVD* and a TV with DVD player

(*Optional:* items from your prop box, a cell phone, popcorn, TV, iPod with speakers, movie snacks)

QUIET ON THE SET

To launch the lesson:
- Welcome everyone to the group. Be sure to use first names or preferred nicknames and introduce visitors. After your students have had time to socialize, pull them in and have them get comfortable.
- Go over your Rules of Engagement, if needed. (See the Rules of Engagement suggestions on p. 6 for more information.)

11: Dirty Dancing

- Review the journaling component you've chosen for your group. (See Create a Group Journal on p. 10 for more information.)

ACTION

Either have students perform the "A Lousy Feeling" skit, watch "A Lousy Feeling" on the *Shocking and Scandalous Stories from the Bible DVD*, or do both. If you choose to have students perform the skit live, give copies of "A Lousy Feeling" (pp. 151, 152) to your student actors and have them prep by reading through their parts a time or two. Also, invite the actors to rummage through the prop box for items to enhance their performance.

> If you want, make a video of your students' live performance of "A Lousy Feeling." Play it back later, perhaps for the entire church.

PLAY BACK

Spend some time reflecting on "A Lousy Feeling" with your entire group by using the questions below. Don't edit your students' responses—allow them to say what they honestly feel. As students talk, have a volunteer record the group's impressions and suggested endings in the journaling component you've chosen. Give every student the opportunity to comment or to journal. Write "A Lousy Feeling" and the date at the top of the journal entry.

OK, now it's time for you to decide how the scenario ends.

> If your group is too small to divide into same-gender groups, handle the discussion questions with sensitivity. You know your students and their maturity level, so you make the call. If you need to, skip questions that may be too difficult for your students to talk about in mixed company.

Use these questions to get a group discussion going:
- In your opinion, did Susan make the right decision inviting Tiffany over? Why or why not?
- How would you rate Tiffany's friendship? a) the best ever!; b) semi-poisonous, but not life threatening; c) drop-kick awful. Why?
- Now that Susan is in this spot, what do you think she'll decide to do?
- What do you think Susan *should* do?
- What do you do when friends make choices that don't consider the situations you are facing?

It's never easy to speak up when you're outnumbered, is it? The pretty party girl in today's PG-13 feature makes several heart-wrenching choices. Watch for them and the devastation that follows in *Dirty Dancing*, up next. ✘

Take 2: Feature Presentation (15 to 20 minutes)

Setup: Your students will take a close look at the story of King Herod, Herodias, and Salome, and discuss why poor decisions led to tragic consequences.

Props: Photocopies of **Outtakes** (p. 153); 4 flip charts on easels or 4 large sheets of paper affixed to the wall; markers or pens

Optional: Bibles

QUIET ON THE SET

Pass out copies of **Outtakes**, one per student. *Optional:* Have students grab their own Bibles.

ACTION

Use **Outtakes** to introduce and teach the Bible story. First, briefly introduce the **Cast** and make sure your students know who's who. Next, use **Movie Trailer** to cover the highlights of the Bible background and story. Then have a volunteer read the Bible story (Mark 6:17-29) out loud from **Outtakes** or have a volunteer read it. If you prefer, have students read the passage from their own Bibles.

PLAY BACK

Label each flip chart with one name: *Herod, John the Baptist, Herodias,* and *Salome.* Then divide your group into two or more small groups for discussion with an adult or older teen leader for each group. If possible, plan to make groups all guys or all girls. Guys will look more closely at King Herod and John the Baptist (Guy Talk) and girls will zero in on Herodias and Salome (Girl Talk). Remind group leaders to be ready to enhance discussion with insights from **Why Is This PG-13 Story in the Bible?** (p. 143).

Have groups record their answers and insights on the flip charts; encourage them to write words or phrases that they think describe each person in the Bible story.

Let's examine the motivations, choices, and consequences we just read about.

11: Dirty Dancing

Guy Talk: Get into the heads of King Herod and John the Baptist.

- **What do you think were Herod's motivations?** *(Fear of losing face; ego; lust; drunkenness; wanting to show off for his friends; lack of self-control; an "I am above the law" attitude)*
- **Do you think suggestive clothes and sensual dancing trigger lust in men? How?**
- **In your opinion, is it fair to blame a guy's lust on a girl's clothes or behaviors? Why or why not?** *(Yes—a guy can't help what thoughts slam into his head if a girl is trying to get his attention! No, it's not fair to blame a guy's problems on somebody else.)*
- **Alcohol inhibits the ability to think clearly and makes wrong choices seem right. Why is this the case? Have you ever seen this happen to people?**
- **What do you think compelled John to call out Herod and Herodias in public? How difficult would this have been? Do you think he had fears to overcome before doing so?**

Girl Talk: Get into the heads of Herodias and Salome.

- **What do you think were Herodias's possible motivations? How about Salome's?** *(Anger; bitterness; jealousy; pride; the intense desire for prestige; position; control; power; manipulation; sensual power; greed; popularity; wanting to please her mother; the need to gain the attention of her powerful stepfather)*
- **How much did gossip (aka "murder by mouth") play into this situation?**
- **Do you think clothing—even when innocently purchased—attracts attention from men that girls and women may not really want? Why is it important to be wise about these choices?**
- **In your opinion, is it fair to blame a guy's lust on a girl's clothes or behaviors? Why or why not?** *(No—girls don't have any control over a guy's thoughts or actions. Yes—sometimes girls are trying to get guys to lust after them.)*
- **What do you think about women using their looks as a tool to get their way? Is this right? Can it lead to sin? Explain your point of view.**

Bring the discussion teams back together. Briefly review discussion results by looking at the four sheets of paper together.

Continue your discussion as a large group by asking questions like:

- **What's your impression of the cast of *Dirty Dancing*?**

SHOCKING AND SCANDALOUS STORIES FROM THE BIBLE

- Do you think the motivations to show off or deceive felt right to King Herod, Herodias, or Salome? Does feeling right make something right? *(Note: this is a great question to spend a little extra time on.)*
- Why do you think this story is in the Bible? *(This is a good time to remind your students of the Key Verse: "Above all else, guard your heart, for it is the wellspring of life" [Proverbs 4:23].)*

Jesus called Herod a "fox" (Luke 13:32), a clue about Herod's sneaky personality. And does it ever play out! Selfish motives and temptation's fulfillment led to terrible choices and behavior within Herod's family. In the end, their hearts' desires led to the death of an innocent and godly man.

Ask the group questions like:

- In your opinion, what were the top three bad choices found in today's story? *(Herod chose to have John the Baptist arrested. Herodias chose to use her daughter to get what she wanted. Salome chose to ask for John the Baptist's head on a platter. Herod chose to honor his alcohol-induced promise.)*
- What were the consequences of each of those choices?
- How could the story have ended if Herod had made a different choice? Herodias? Salome? John the Baptist?

Today's feature spiraled downward to a gruesome final act. God's point of view is obvious: Your heart is impressionable; guard it with everything you have. ✘

Take 3: Critics' Corner (15 to 20 minutes)

Setup: Reinforce the points you want your students to take away from today's lesson.
Props: Group journal with entries from Take 1; **Outtakes** (p. 153); individual snack-size M&M or Skittle candy bags (about 2 bags per student), 2 or more large bowls

QUIET ON THE SET

Grab the group journal and have students circle up to review the alternative endings for the "A Lousy Feeling" skit recorded in the group journal.

ACTION

Consider God's POV

Ask the group:

- Fast-forward five years for Salome. How do you think she'd be feeling about herself?
- In retrospect, how might she judge her behavior at Herod's party?

Draw students' attention to the **POV** on the **Outtakes** handout: *Be careful what you allow into your heart; influences turn into actions with final consequences.*

Have a volunteer read the alternative endings for the "A Lousy Feeling" skit from the group journal. After each entry is read, ask your students to stand up if they think the ending reflects the POV.

Once all of the entries have been read, have students vote to select the ending they think best reflects today's POV. (If none of the endings from the journal seem to fit, help the group write a new one.)

Understand God's Truth

We've had a lot of great discussion. Let's go back over a couple of things.

Ask the group:

- **What have we learned from today's story?** *(Herod followed the influences of his wife and his guests, not God. We hurt ourselves and others when we give in to pressure from others and make choices that are not God-centered.)*
- **What positive influences help you make godly choices?** *(Stay in the Word; go to church; connect with friends that respect you and your choices.)*

Christians face situations that require courage. John the Baptist was in such a situation. In her own way, Susan was too.

Teamwork

It's important to be a visible example of God to the world. Otherwise, how will others know what's in our hearts? Together we can make a memorable imprint.

PLAY BACK

Wrap up the meeting with a team-building game that helps students learn to rely on each other. Then close in prayer.

Food Court Race

Needed: individual snack-size M&M or Skittle candy bags, about 12 for every team of 6 to 8 students; 2 large bowls

Goal: Fill the bowl with candy bags using feet only!

Verse-atility: *I'll keep watch over my heart; I'll need it to make great choices.*

How to Play:

Have players take off their shoes and form two or more teams; ideally, each team should have six to eight members. Direct teams to each form a line, then have students lie back on the floor with their feet up. Place a bowl next to the last person at the end of each line.

Team leaders start the game by placing one snack-size candy bag on the feet of the person closest to them. Teams pass the bags down the line from one set of feet to the other. If the candy bag drops along the way, play starts over for that team. The last player in line must drop the bags into his or her team's bowl. If the bag misses, the player must feel for it, press it between his or her toes, and try again to drop it into the bowl. (If your group is small, you can play as one team or have students pass the candy up and down the line to see how dexterous they get.)

Want to really challenge your group? Place the bowl at a distance from the last student. The last-in-line player must "shoot for the basket" and, if they miss, roll over to where the bag is, pick it up, and return for another shot. (You might make two misses the maximum so you're not there all night!) The team to fill their bowl first wins—and gets to choose the candy, snack, or pizza next time you have food.

After the game, say: **We needed each other to keep the candy moving just like we need each other to guard against bad influences and make God-pleasing choices.**

Close with Prayer

Ask your group to look again at **Outtakes** and repeat today's **Key Verse:** "Above all else, guard your heart, for it is the wellspring of life" (Proverbs 4:23). Then point out this week's *Verse-atility: I'll keep watch over my heart; I'll need it to make great choices.* If time permits, jot the verse in the group journal and have everyone initial it.

Invite students to share prayer requests, then pray together. ✘

A Lousy Feeling

Characters:
NARRATOR
SUSAN: a young teen girl
TIFFANY: Susan's friend
TEENS: several guys and girls (4 to 6) who come to Susan's house, uninvited; mostly nonspeaking parts
Scene: Susan is home alone; her parents went out to dinner.
Prop Suggestions: Select any props or costumes you want from the prop box. Also, if you want, use a cell phone, popcorn, TV, and iPod with speakers (or just pretend!).
Director's Note: The Narrator's part, below, is delivered by Susan on the *Shocking and Scandalous Stories from the Bible DVD.*

SCRIPT

NARRATOR:
Susan couldn't believe the house was hers. No twin brother to deal with, and Mom and Dad had gone out to dinner for the evening. The whole house was hers. She loved this feeling.

(Susan's getting the popcorn out of the microwave when her cell phone rings. Susan answers it.)

SUSAN:
Hey.

TIFFANY:
(voice on the line, from off stage:) Hey, it's me. I'm coming by. I thought we'd play some video games or something. Cool?

NARRATOR:
Susan bites her lip and thinks.

(Susan portrays deep—but quick—thought.)

As much as she'd love to say "Cool!", she knows her parents' rule: no friends can come over when her parents aren't home.

SUSAN:
Uh . . . yeah. Uh . . . sure, come on over. Popcorn's ready.

TIFFANY:
You rock, girl. Be over in a minute.

SUSAN:
See ya.

NARRATOR:
Tiffany hangs up the phone and stands there, thinking: *Mom and Dad can't get that mad. It's just Tiffany.* She reaches to get her popcorn . . .

A FEW MINUTES LATER . . .

(Tiffany lets herself in the front door and several other teens follow her inside.)

Without bothering to knock, Tiffany comes through the front door. Susan's about to get her something to drink when she notices . . . six other teens, a few from high school, but two or three who Susan has never met.

(Susan appears very uneasy with the crowd that's come in her house.)

Susan is thinking to herself, *How could she do this to me? **What is she thinking?** I don't even know some of these guys.*

TIFFANY:
(walking into the kitchen to meet Susan, then giving her a funny grin) **Hey, why don't you go up and change, Susan? Grab that cute little outfit we got you last week.**

SUSAN:
What outfit?

TIFFANY:
You know . . . You're too funny. Come on.

SUSAN:
(thinking to herself, but speaking out loud while turning to the audience:) **Mom made me return them—she said they made me look 'older,' too much older. Not what someone my age should wear. But I can't tell Tiffany that. Not *now*. She was acting weird. I'd never seen her act like this.**

(Tiffany goes back to the living room and turns up her iPod and starts to dance while looking in Caleb's direction.)

NARRATOR:
Meanwhile, Tiffany starts into some dance moves. It's obvious that she's looking in Caleb's direction, hoping he'll notice.
Susan is getting a little more nervous by the minute and wishes she could just run upstairs, fall in bed, and pretend that this is all just a bad dream.

(Tiffany continues to dance while listening to her iPod and glancing with flirting looks toward another guy.)

SUSAN:
(thinking to herself, but speaking out loud while turning to the audience:)
I've never seen Tiffany act this way. What is she doing? If she doesn't quit, she'll get in trouble. We'll both get in trouble.

NARRATOR:
Susan needs to figure a way out of this. But how?

SUSAN:
(thinking to herself, but speaking out loud while turning to the audience:) **If I ask everyone to leave, I'll never hear the end of it. They'll laugh in my face. I'll never live it down. This was not what I had in mind for this night. What a mess.**

NARRATOR:
What Susan thought would be a great time with her friend has suddenly turned into something very different.

(Susan's cell phone rings—the sound of an incoming text message. Susan jumps. She picks it up and reads the text.)

SUSAN:
(thinking to herself, but speaking out loud while turning to the audience:)
It's Mom—her text says the restaurant was packed, and they just grabbed some pizza and are heading home. They'll be here in a couple of minutes. . . . *What do I do now?!?*

(The skit ends with a look of panic on Susan's face as the others dance, laugh, or watch TV in the background.)

(Actors rejoin group.)

Permission is granted by Standard Publishing to reproduce this "A Lousy Feeling" script for ministry purposes only (not for resale).

Outtakes

CAST
King Herod (Herod Antipas): ruler of Galilee and Perea; while still married to wife #1, marries his brother's wife, Herodias

Herodias: married to Philip; leaves Philip to marry Herod

Salome: Herodias and Philip's daughter

John the Baptist: a courageous and righteous man of God

MOVIE TRAILER
- Herodias leaves her first marriage to marry Herod.
- John the Baptist boldly declares that this marriage is unlawful.
- Herod has John arrested.
- Herod throws a birthday party—for himself.
- Herodias's daughter, historically known as Salome, dances for the drunken men.
- The princess's sexy dance turns Herod's head.
- Herod grants Salome any request she desires.
- After speaking with her mother, Salome asks for John the Baptist to be beheaded.

Verse-atility: I'll keep watch over my heart; I'll need it to make great choices.

POV: Be careful what you allow into your heart; influences turn into actions with final consequences.

Key Verse: Above all else, guard your heart, for it is the wellspring of life (Proverbs 4:23).

DIRTY DANCING
Mark 6:17-29 (*The Message*)
(*We've added a few of our own comments in* **bold** *below.*)

Herod was the one who had ordered the arrest of John, put him in chains, and sent him to prison at the nagging of Herodias, his brother Philip's wife. For John had provoked Herod by naming his relationship with Herodias "adultery." Herodias, smoldering with hate, wanted to kill him, but didn't dare because Herod was in awe of John. Convinced that he was a holy man, he gave him special treatment. Whenever he listened to him he was miserable with guilt **[you don't say?]**—and yet he couldn't stay away. Something in John kept pulling him back.

But a portentous day arrived when Herod threw a birthday party, inviting all the brass and bluebloods in Galilee. Herodias's daughter **[party girl]** entered the banquet hall and danced for the guests. She dazzled Herod and the guests.

The king said to the girl, "Ask me anything. I'll give you anything you want." Carried away, he kept on, "I swear, I'll split my kingdom with you if you say so!"

She went back to her mother and said, "What should I ask for?"

"Ask for the head of John the Baptizer."

Excited, she ran back to the king and said, "I want the head of John the Baptizer served up on a platter. And I want it now!"

That sobered the king up fast. But unwilling to lose face with his guests, he caved in and let her have her wish. The king sent the executioner off to the prison with orders to bring back John's head. He went, cut off John's head, brought it back on a platter, and presented it to the girl, who gave it to her mother. **[Seriously gross and tragic.]**

When's John's disciples heard about this, they came and got the body and gave it a decent burial.

Permission is granted by Standard Publishing to reproduce this **Outtakes** handout for ministry purposes only (not for resale).

12 The Mob

Director's Commentary

NOW SHOWING: *The Mob*

FROM THE BIBLE: The stoning of Stephen (Acts 6:8-15; 7:54-60).

RATED PG-13 FOR: witness tampering and mob hysteria leading to a violent death

POV: Don't let negative peer pressure determine your choices.

KEY VERSE: "Do not follow the crowd in doing wrong" (Exodus 23:2).

The Lesson	Time	What you'll do . . .	How you'll do it . . .	What you'll need . . .
Take 1: Preview	15 to 20 minutes	Start off your lesson by introducing the theme with a relational, creative activity.	Option 1: Students create wristbands and discuss social pressure.	Photocopies of "Trash Talk Wristband Instructions" (p. 164); old magazines, scissors, glue, tape, hole punch, colorful beads, twist ties, yarn or string, a variety of simple recyclables; thin rope; group journal supplies, markers
			Option 2: Students watch a DVD version of "Cool? Uncool?" and discuss it. Or, choose to do both.	*Shocking and Scandalous Stories from the Bible DVD,* TV, and DVD player
Take 2: Feature Presentation	15 to 20 minutes	Dive into the Bible story and explore it together.	Small group and large group discussion	Photocopies of **Outtakes** (p. 165); white garbage bags, permanent markers *Optional:* Bibles, scissors
Take 3: Critics' Corner	15 to 20 minutes	Help your students grasp God's point of view and wrap things up with a fun team-building activity.	Discussion, game, and prayer	**Outtakes** handouts; group journal; 2 or more lemons, 2 or more pencils, masking tape, string, or yarn

Why Is This PG-13 Story in the Bible?

When the Holy Spirit first came to Christians in Jerusalem, the number of believers shot up. Stephen was one of seven administrators appointed to look after the needs of these Christians (Acts 6:5), but he also used other gifts. In Acts 6, Stephen is infectiously spreading the good news. God's Spirit has also allowed Stephen to perform miracles. If the sermons don't make heads turn, the miracles certainly do. One particular pocket of Jews gets ticked off. These are the "Freedmen"—Jews who were freed slaves from various parts of the Roman Empire. They banded together in Jerusalem to open their own meeting place. They're all about following the Jewish party line, and Stephen is trouble.

The Freedmen debate what Stephen is preaching and doing—but he's too smart for them. Whatever they say, he has a good answer. So they ratchet things up by bribing a couple of guys to say things about Stephen that twist the truth. The next thing you know, Stephen and the witnesses are standing before the Jewish High Council, where the witnesses repeat their lies and Stephen is charged with blasphemy—speaking against God himself. This incites the mob, who want justice (as they define it)—and they want it *now*.

> **Connecting with Community**
> Log on to www.shockingandscandalous.com to connect with other ministries:
> - Check out a sample video of other students in action.
> - Share with other leaders at the PG-13 forum about what's working in your ministry, what's not, or how you used *Shocking and Scandalous* this week.
> - Or ask for input about other aspects of middle school ministry.

Supposedly Stephen is on trial, but the whole business is a charade. The Jewish legal system had a process to safeguard someone accused of blasphemy. At the very least, the person would have an opportunity to deny the charge or, if the charge was accurate, publicly change his mind. Stephen does have a chance to speak in his own defense, which he uses to call listeners to repentance (Acts 7:2-53). This is not what the crowd wants to hear. That's the end of any semblance of judicial order. The mob scene hurtles straight to the penalty for blasphemy—death by stoning. When a person was stoned in that culture, he was pushed off a ledge. If he survived the fall, someone would drop a stone on his chest. If he was still alive, others would begin throwing stones.

No one comes to Stephen's defense. No one is interested in justice. Stephen pays the ultimate price for his faith.

Jesus was killed following a charge of blasphemy and prayed for God to forgive those who crucified him. Like Jesus, Stephen also dies with a prayer of forgiveness on his lips. His death makes him the first person to literally give his life for the good news. The event ignited the first all-out wave of persecution against Christians who were answering a radical call from God.

This story of the power of a mob will help middle schoolers realize that following Jesus often means standing alone in a self-righteous "me" crowd.

Take It to Your Students

Here are some key points to put in front of your students with this lesson:
- Getting carried away with the crowd is no guarantee you're doing the right thing.
- Don't follow the crowd because of the social rewards.
- Harmful peer pressure—whether a mob or one friend—doesn't have to determine your choices. ✘

The Mob: The Lesson

Take 1: Preview (15 to 20 minutes)

Setup: This activity will set up the day's Bible story in a relational way as students make eco-friendly wristbands and discuss how others might judge them.

Props: Group journal supplies, markers; photocopies of "Trash Talk Wristband Instructions" (p. 164); scissors, glue, tape, hole punch, colorful beads, twist ties, yarn or string, thin rope, a variety of simple recyclables (such as old magazines, nutrition or granola bar wrappers, candy papers, shiny gum wrappers, junk mail, and so on)

Optional: Shocking and Scandalous Stories from the Bible DVD, TV, and DVD player

QUIET ON THE SET

To launch the lesson:
- Welcome everyone to the group. Use first names or preferred nicknames and introduce visitors. After your students have had some time to socialize, pull them in and have them get comfortable.

12: The Mob

- Go over your Rules of Engagement, if needed. (See the Rules of Engagement suggestions on p. 6 for more information.)
- Review the journaling component you've chosen for your group. (See Create a Group Journal on p. 10 for more information.)

ACTION

Spread out the recyclables and other supplies as well as several copies of the "Trash Talk Wristband Instructions" handouts.

Let's imagine that an eco-conscious company has contracted our group. Wasteables, Inc. wants us to design a new series of wristbands exclusively for young teens and preteens—all made from recyclable materials.

Have your students use their imaginations to make creative wristbands from the recyclable material you provide. They can use the "Trash Talk Wristband Instructions" to guide them or come up with their own ideas. When they're done, invite students to model their wristbands.

> For fun, you can have your students plan a mock TV commercial featuring various views of the wristbands and some simple descriptive commentary. If you choose this option, take video of the mock commercial and play it back later. Or play it for parents or the whole church to display your students' filmmaking capabilities.

PLAY BACK

Talk about the materials used in the wristbands. Ask:

- **Time to put it out there. How would your new recycled look go over at school? Would you face ridicule or judgment from some for wearing "trash"?**

Allow your group to share honestly, then discuss their responses.

Have a volunteer record the group's thoughts on peer pressure. Be sure to date the entry and give it a title like "Trash Talk." As always, encourage all students to participate with the journal, even if it's just to initial in agreement.

> If you have time and want to get your students moving around, designate one wall as "cool" and another as "uncool." Then name various hobbies, foods, styles, movies, and so on. Students must vote on each item, designating it as either cool or uncool, by moving to the appropriate wall. Encourage your students to be true to their own opinion and not just follow the crowd when they vote.

It was fun to "think green" and create something new from something old. Still, if others don't see our designs quite the way we do, we might be tempted to change our minds.

DVD Option: Show your group the "Cool? Uncool?" video from the *Shocking and Scandalous Stories from the Bible DVD*. After the video, continue with the discussion below.

Ask the group:
- In your opinion, what makes something cool? What makes something uncool? Give examples.
- What's the coolest thing you own?
- If somebody asked you "What's the most uncool thing on the planet?," what would you say? Why?

Now let's go a bit deeper . . .
- Who decides what's cool or uncool?
- What bothers you most about peer pressure?
- Have you ever witnessed a group turn on someone? How did it make you feel?

Popularity usually means having social power and leverage over others. Grade yourself (A, B, C, etc.) on how well you do in keeping this desire in check.

Allow students a moment to privately think about their grade.

Mobsource is what we could call the theme of today's peer pressure/trash talk lesson. Simply put, mobsource is the strong pull to belong, to be accepted and connected, and to look, think, and be part of the crowd in power.

Mobsource spikes fear and chaos in today's PG-13 New Testament feature. And it's as bad as it gets. A plot to kill in *The Mob*, up next. ✘

Take 2: Feature Presentation (15 to 20 minutes)

Setup: Your students will take a close look at the story of Stephen being stoned and discuss what it takes to resist peer pressure.

Props: Photocopies of **Outtakes** (p. 165); white garbage bags, permanent markers

Optional: Bibles, scissors

12: The Mob

QUIET ON THE SET

Pass out copies of **Outtakes**, one per student. *Optional:* Have students grab their own Bibles.

ACTION

Use **Outtakes** to introduce and teach the Bible story. First, briefly introduce the **Cast** and make sure your students know who's who. Next, use **Movie Trailer** to cover the highlights of the Bible background and story. Then read the Bible story (Acts 6:8-15; 7:54-60) out loud from **Outtakes** or have a volunteer read it. (If you prefer, ask students to read the passage aloud from their own Bibles.)

PLAY BACK

Divide your group into two or more small teams for discussion with an adult or older teen leader for each group. Assign roughly half the teams to discuss the point of view of the Freedmen and the mob (Team Talk 1); have the remaining teams talk about things from Stephen's perspective (Team Talk 2). Remind group leaders to be ready to enhance discussion with insights from **Why Is This PG-13 Story in the Bible?** (p. 155).

> Have students use the sealed edge of each garbage bag as the top of the "page."

Give each small group a couple of white garbage bags and permanent markers. Have students use the Team Talk questions to discuss the motivations they see in the story characters and then write their thoughts on the trash bags.

Critical evidence. Let's examine the damage peer pressure can do by writing our thoughts on these trash bags.

> Team Talk 1: Get into the heads of the Freedmen and the mob.

- **What do you think was the motivation behind what the Freedmen did?** *(Religious belief, jealousy, hatred)*
- **How did they trash-talk Stephen? What was the result?** *(They twisted his words and lied about him. They made him seem like somebody who was preaching against God.)*
- **Like a magnet, a *mobsource* attracts others. Why is the pull so strong?** *(It's easy to get wrapped up in the emotions of a crowd. People want others to like them—they want to please others—so they do what the others do.)*
- **Do you blame the mob for getting carried away? Why or why not?**

Team Talk 2: Get into the head of Stephen.

- **What do you think was the motivation behind the preaching and miracles Stephen did?** *(Stephen knew the truth and couldn't back down. He was spreading the good news about Jesus.)*
- **What do you make of Stephen's vision of heaven? Why do you think God gave him that vision in his last moments?** *(It would probably comfort him. Even under the pain of death, it showed he was right.)*
- **In your opinion, what impact did Stephen want to have on the crowd?** *(He dared to speak the truth, and that made them uncomfortable.)*
- **What do you think was the motivation behind Stephen's last words?** *(The gospel in action—forgiveness)*

Bring the discussion teams back together. Review discussion results by looking at what's written on the trash bags.

Option: Cut a head hole in the sealed edge of the bags and have volunteers wear the bags during the review.

Continue your discussion as a large group by asking questions like:

- **Front and center: How do you see negative peer pressure at work in today's story?**
- **Behind the scenes: How do you see truth at work in this story?**
- **What does this story have to do with you?**
- **How can you honor the uniqueness of the teens and preteens you know?**

Stephen could have played it safe. He could have gone home, put his feet up, and led a quiet life. Instead he spoke the unpopular truth about Jesus to those who didn't want to hear it.

Ask the group questions like:

- **Can one person make a difference for good? Share an example of somebody you know or have heard about.**
- **Where in this story could things have turned out differently?**
- **Why do you think this story is in the Bible?** *(This is an opportunity to remind your students of today's Key Verse: "Do not follow the crowd in doing wrong" [Exodus 23:2].)*

12: The Mob

Stephen's words angered an already furious crowd. Yet, the truth had to be said. Negative peer pressure doesn't have to determine your choices. Admittedly, it's not easy. An unpopular stance for right takes courage—along with a pounding heart and sweaty palms. ✘

Take 3: Critics' Corner (15 to 20 minutes)

Setup: Reinforce the points you want your students to take away from today's lesson.

Props: Group journal with entries from Take 1; **Outtakes** (p. 165); 2 or more lemons, 2 or more pencils, masking tape, string, or yarn (to mark lanes)

QUIET ON THE SET

Grab the group journal and ask students to review the day's earlier entries on the criticism their new recycled wristbands might receive at school.

ACTION

Consider the POV

Ask the group:

- What are you most afraid of when standing up for yourself or for your beliefs? Is your fear realistic? Why or why not?
- Can you "fix" peer pressure? Why or why not? *(Note: have a volunteer jot down responses in the group journal.)*
- If I said, "One in three middle schoolers today believe it's OK to pick on unpopular kids in school," would this be true or false? Why? If true, how can you help?
- Positive pressure: What if a few people from today's mob had come to Stephen's defense? How might the story have had a happier ending?

Love cares for others. Love is not a mob or crowd with a hurtful agenda. Make a power choice.

Have students grab their Bibles and read 1 Corinthians 13 to themselves. Allow some time for them to reflect on the passage.

Draw your students' attention to the **POV** on the **Outtakes** handout: *Don't let peer pressure determine your choices.* Emphasize the importance of this idea.

Understand God's Truth

Stephen endured a mob's backlash and paid the ultimate price. There's also a price to pay when we neglect God's holy ways for popularity. Don't let hurtful peer pressure determine your choices.

Ask the group:

- **What have we learned from today's story?** *(False witnesses fueled a mob's anger, resulting in Stephen's death.)*
- **If you could step into today's Bible story and change one thing, what would it be? Explain.** *(Come to Stephen's aid; don't compromise my beliefs; I won't allow the crowd to determine what's best for me.)*

Teamwork

Dual existence. Just like the mob in today's story, we too often resist the truth if it's inconvenient or makes us uncomfortable or unpopular. But remember, we're a community. We don't have to go it alone! We have the power to strengthen each other—to help each other stand up to the crowd. Let's be there for each other this week through prayer and positive action.

PLAY BACK

Wrap up the meeting with a team-building game that helps players think about not wobbling in their choices. Then close in prayer.

The Grand Prix

Needed: lemons, pencils, game lanes from tape, string, or yarn
Goal: Roll lemons down the lane as quickly as possible.

How to Play:

Divide your group into two or more even teams. Use masking tape, string, or yarn to create two or more lanes on the floor. Have teams divide in half, then line up in single file at both ends of their assigned lane. At one end, hand the first players in line a lemon and a pencil. The object of the game is to roll the lemon down the lane using the pencil; the player at the other end then rolls it back. (This is not as easy as it sounds because of the lemon's odd shape!) Lemons must stay in assigned lanes or that leg starts over for that team! Play continues back and forth until all team members have completed the activity. Encourage players to cheer each other on.

After the game, say: **As you leave today, think about how wobbly your choices are when you submit to the not-so-great direction of the in-crowd. Better idea? Choose to live by God's ways instead!**

> If your group is small, line up players on one end only. Have them roll the lemon down and back to the next team player.

Close with Prayer

Ask your group to look again at **Outtakes** and repeat today's **Key Verse:** "Do not follow the crowd in doing wrong" (Exodus 23:2). Then point out today's *Verse-atility: I don't have to be a crowd-pleaser for wrong.* Encourage your students to keep God's truth front and center in their lives this week. If time permits, jot the verse in the group journal and have everyone initial it.

Invite students to share prayer requests, especially about standing up to peer pressure.

Stephen died with a prayer of forgiveness on his lips.

Encourage students to be like Stephen—lead them in praying for others at school who put peer pressure on them. Then pray for students' other requests. ✘

> **Verse-atility:** *I don't have to be a crowd-pleaser for wrong.*

Trash Talk Wristband Instructions

Here is a super-simple wristband idea . . .

STEP 1: Tear out a page from an old magazine.

STEP 2: Accordion-fold the page lengthwise.

STEP 3: Bring the ends of the folded page together and overlap a bit.

STEP 4: Hole-punch the overlapped section and secure your new wristband with a twist tie or string. Before twisting or knotting ends closed, insert a few beads for color.

STEP 5: If you choose, glue on colorful candy wrappers folded into squares or shiny gum wrappers folded into stars.

Slip on your new wristband. Now, use your imagination (you can also braid, knot, or weave magazine strips together), and take it from here!

OR TRY THIS IDEA . . .

Have your students cut string, yarn, or thin rope into bracelets that fit their wrists. Let them use beads or any other decorations they wish. These will be like the friendship bracelets that many young people wear.

Permission is granted by Standard Publishing to reproduce "Trash Talk Wristband Instructions" for ministry purposes only (not for resale).

Outtakes

CAST
Stephen: a follower of Jesus, preaching about him and doing miracles
Freedmen: don't like what Stephen is saying about Moses and the temple
Religious leaders: not fond of people who followed Jesus

MOVIE TRAILER
- Stephen is filled with the Holy Spirit and doing miracles.
- Freedmen (members of a Jewish group) argue with Stephen, but they can't win.
- Freedmen decide to get rid of Stephen by paying people to lie and accuse him of cursing God.
- The liars tell their lies to the religious leaders and stir up an angry crowd against Stephen.
- The mob kills Stephen without a fair trial, but Stephen prays for God to forgive them.

Verse-atility: I don't have to be a crowd-pleaser for wrong.

POV: Don't let negative peer pressure determine your choices.
Key Verse: Do not follow the crowd in doing wrong (Exodus 23:2).

Gang Violence
Acts 6:8-15; 7:54-60 *(The Message)*
*(We've added a few of our own comments **in bold** below.)*

Stephen, brimming with God's grace and energy, was doing wonderful things among the people, unmistakable signs that God was among them. But then some men from the meeting place whose membership was made up of freed slaves, Cyrenians, Alexandrians, and some others from Cilicia and Asia, went up against him trying to argue him down. But they were no match for his wisdom and spirit when he spoke.

So in secret they bribed men to lie: "We heard him cursing Moses and God."

That stirred up the people, the religious leaders, and religion scholars. They grabbed Stephen and took him before the High Council. They put forward their bribed witnesses to testify: "This man talks nonstop against this Holy Place and God's Law. We even heard him say that Jesus of Nazareth would tear this place down and throw out all the customs Moses gave us." **[Close . . . but not quite.]**

As all those who sat on the High Council looked at Stephen, they found they couldn't take their eyes off him—his face was like the face of an angel!

[Stephen used the opportunity to preach once more about Jesus, but the crowd didn't want to hear that they should repent.]

. . . At that point they went wild, a rioting mob of catcalls and whistles and invective. But Stephen, full of the Holy Spirit, hardly noticed—he only had eyes for God, whom he saw in all his glory with Jesus standing at his side. He said, "Oh! I see heaven wide open and the Son of Man standing at God's side!"

Yelling and hissing, the mob drowned him out. Now in full stampede, they dragged him out of town and pelted him with rocks. The ringleaders took off their coats and asked a young man named Saul to watch them.

As the rocks rained down, Stephen prayed, "Master Jesus, take my life." Then he knelt down, praying loud enough for everyone to hear, "Master, don't blame them for this sin"—his last words. Then he died.

Permission is granted by Standard Publishing to reproduce this **Outtakes** handout for ministry purposes only (not for resale).

13 Under the Influence

Director's Commentary

NOW SHOWING: *Under the Influence*

FROM THE BIBLE: Simon the sorcerer tries to buy God's gift (Acts 8:9-24).

RATED PG-13 FOR: God-complex behavior and attempting to buy the power of the Holy Spirit

POV: Money can't buy the powerful gifts God gives us.

KEY VERSE: "All these are the work of one and the same Spirit, and he gives them to each one, just as he determines" (1 Corinthians 12:11).

The Lesson	Time	What you'll do...	How you'll do it...	What you'll need...
Take 1: Preview	15 to 20 minutes	Start off your lesson by introducing the theme with a relational, creative activity.	Option 1: Students talk about money in a game of hot seat.	Photocopy of "Money, Money, Money" (p. 175) cut into slips, basket or bowl; group journal supplies, markers
			Option 2: Students watch a DVD version of "Money, Money, Money" and discuss it. Or, choose to do both.	*Shocking and Scandalous Stories from the Bible DVD*, TV, and DVD player
Take 2: Feature Presentation	15 to 20 minutes	Dive into the Bible story and explore it together.	Small group and large group discussion	Photocopies of **Outtakes** (p. 176), play money bills; dark markers (*Optional:* Bibles, tape, poster board)
Take 3: Critics' Corner	15 to 20 minutes	Help your students grasp God's point of view and wrap things up with a fun team-building activity.	Discussion, game, and prayer	**Outtakes** handouts; group journal, red marker; small trinket

Why Is This PG-13 Story in the Bible?

The death of Stephen in Acts 7 is the beginning of open season on Christians, who are hounded and bullied and killed for their faith. Believers, who had been concentrated in Jerusalem, scatter and carry the gospel with them. Philip goes to Samaria, preaches about God's kingdom, performs miracles, and gathers a following. The city is enthralled with their experience of God, and it seems that Philip displaces the popularity of a famous practitioner of magical arts named Simon. Now Philip is casting out demons and healing paralyzed people and making a general ruckus with Simon's audience. Acts 8:13 says that even Simon believes and is baptized. He follows Philip everywhere, astonished at what he is doing.

Later Peter and John arrive, sent by the apostles in Jerusalem to check out the reports about Samaria. When Peter and John lay their hands on the Samaritans and pray, the Spirit comes to the Samaritans. That's Simon's cue to jump right in. Simon knows a get-rich-quick scheme when he sees one. Just think of the fortune he could make if he had this kind of power! Out comes his money clip; he'll pay any price for the ability to do what Peter and John just did. He can make a fortune charging for using that gift.

> **Connecting with Community**
> Log on to www.shockingand scandalous.com to connect with other ministries:
> - Check out a sample video of other students in action.
> - Share with other leaders at the PG-13 forum about what's working in your ministry, what's not, or how you used *Shocking and Scandalous* this week.
> - Or ask for input about other aspects of middle school ministry.

Peter is furious. How dare Simon think that God's gift can be reduced to something to be bartered! Simon is trying to get in on the action, but instead, Peter says that with this strategy Simon will never have a part in what God is doing. God's gifts are not for sale. Simon has to turn inside out and ask forgiveness.

Did Simon really believe in Jesus? Only God knows. But he may simply have been trying to remain popular in the wake of Philip's ministry, which was distracting his audience. Various stories about Simon circulated outside the Bible. Most likely they are legend, but none of them speaks positively of Simon, who apparently continued to stir up questionable doctrine. The early church fathers regarded him as the first heretic and the father of all heresy.

This Bible story will help middle schoolers see that the power of God's Spirit is not some sort of a magic trick; it comes only through a relationship of faith in Jesus.

SHOCKING AND SCANDALOUS STORIES FROM THE BIBLE

Take It to Your Students

Here are some key points to put in front of your students with this lesson:
- God's Spirit comes to us through a relationship of faith in Jesus.
- We can't manipulate God's power for our own purposes.
- God's gifts are just that—gifts. We can't buy them, sell them, trade them, or earn them. ✗

Under the Influence: The Lesson

Take 1: Preview (15 to 20 minutes)

Setup: This activity will set up the day's Bible story in a relational way as students answer hot seat questions about the powerful allure of money.

Set design: Place a chair set apart from the group; also cut apart and fold the "Money, Money, Money" slips (p. 175), then place them all in a basket or bowl.

Props: Photocopy of "Money, Money, Money" (p. 175) cut into slips, basket or bowl; group journal supplies, markers

Optional: Shocking and Scandalous Stories from the Bible DVD, TV, and DVD player

QUIET ON THE SET

To launch the lesson:
- Welcome everyone to the group. Use first names or preferred nicknames and introduce visitors. After your students have had some time to socialize, pull them in and have them get comfortable.
- Go over your Rules of Engagement, if needed. (See the Rules of Engagement suggestions on p. 6 for more information.)
- Review the journaling method you've chosen for your group. (See Create a Group Journal on p. 10 for more information.)

ACTION

DVD Option: Start this activity off by showing your group the "Money, Money, Money" video from the *Shocking and Scandalous Stories from the Bible DVD* before you lead the hot seat activity below.

Ask your students to gather and draw their attention to the extra chair. Explain that this is the hot seat. Whoever is sitting in the hot seat will draw a question from the bowl. He or she must honestly answer that question and then explain their answer.

13: Under the Influence

Pick a student to sit in the hot seat and begin.

There are ten "Money, Money, Money" slips (taken from the first reproducible at the end of this lesson). After your group goes through all ten, fold them up and put them back in the bowl for the remaining students to draw from.

As various students sit in the hot seat, jot down their answers in the group journal. Be sure to date the entry and give it a creative title.

PLAY BACK

Spend time reflecting together on the hot seat answers. Invite students to discuss each other's responses. Allow your group to share without criticism or critique. Have a volunteer record the group's impressions near the original answers in the journal. As always, encourage all students to participate with the journal, even if it's just to initial in agreement.

We have lots of ideas on money and how it makes our lives easier. Sometimes we go too far in thinking that money is the answer.

Use these questions to continue the discussion:

- What does having money mean to you?
- In your opinion, how much is a lot of money? How much is a lot for somebody your age to have?
- What do you like most about money now that you're older and you have some of your own?
- In your opinion, what is the most valuable thing on earth that money can buy?
- Can money buy you happiness?

Challenge students to defend their answer to the last question, providing examples to explain their reasoning.

Money has power. It can influence others and buy us comfort. But it's garbage when compared with the transforming power of the Holy Spirit. Money meets magic in today's PG-13 feature presentation, *Under the Influence*. ✘

Take 2: Feature Presentation (15 to 20 minutes)

Setup: Your students will take a close look at the story of Simon the sorcerer and discuss the value of God's gift of the Spirit.

Props: Photocopies of **Outtakes** (p. 176); play money bills, dark markers (*Optional:* Bibles, tape, poster board)

QUIET ON THE SET

Pass out copies of **Outtakes,** one per student. *Optional:* Have students grab their own Bibles.

> To keep students hopping, use random methods to determine who will sit in the hot seat next. Some methods include: choose the person who has the next birthday; choose the tallest student; choose the student with the most letters in his or her first name; choose the student who is wearing socks with the most colors.

ACTION

Use **Outtakes** to introduce and teach the Bible story. First, briefly introduce the **Cast** and make sure your students know who's who. Next, use **Movie Trailer** to cover the highlights of the Bible background and story. Then read the Bible story (Acts 8:9-24) out loud from **Outtakes** or have a volunteer read it. If you prefer, ask students to read it from their own Bibles.

PLAY BACK

Divide your group into two or more small teams for discussion with an adult or older teen leader for each group. Have about half the groups talk about Simon's role in the story (Team Talk 1), while the remaining groups look at things from Peter and John's perspective (Team Talk 2). Remind group leaders to be ready to enhance discussion with insights from **Why Is This PG-13 Story in the Bible?** (p. 167).

> If you want, make a video of your group doing the hot seat activity. Play it back later, or play it for the whole church! (But only with your kids' permission.)

Give each group a supply of play money bills and markers. Have students discuss and write about the motivations they see in the story characters on the play money.

Let's take a look at actions and motivations.

Team Talk 1: Get into the head of Simon.

- **How does Simon's past influence what he thought when Peter and John prayed for God's Spirit?** *(He is used to doing tricks and wanted this special gift to go along with his other abilities.)*

13: Under the Influence

- What do you think Simon really wants when he tries to buy this power?
- Do you feel sympathy for Simon in this story? Why or why not?
- What's the main thing that Simon doesn't understand? *(God's power is not for sale.)*

Team Talk 2: Get into the heads of Peter and John.

- What do Peter and John do for the people in Samaria? Why? *(Lay hands on them and pray for them to receive the Holy Spirit.)*
- What do you make of Peter's reaction when Simon wants to buy the gift God had given him? Do you think Peter goes overboard? Why or why not? *(Shock, anger, correction)*
- What's the real issue behind Peter's anger? *(God's gifts are not for sale, including the Spirit.)*
- How does Peter's reaction show that he cares about Simon? *(He tells Simon to ask for forgiveness.)*

Bring the groups back together. Briefly review the results of discussion. If you'd like, tape the play money in the group journal, on the wall, or on a piece of poster board.

Continue your discussion as a large group by asking questions like:

- Is what Simon does in the story really so wrong? Explain.
- How does Simon's attitude show that he doesn't understand what God is doing?
- If Simon were right here with us, what would you explain to him?

God graciously gave the Holy Spirit to the Christians in Jerusalem. Then through Peter and John, God gave the gift of the Holy Spirit to the Samaritans. The Holy Spirit is God's *gift*. It can't be manufactured, distributed, or sold. Simon was out of line when he tried to gain this supernatural ability for himself.

Let's look again at the key choices in this story.

Ask the group questions like:

- What choices did Simon make that changed the story? *(He tried to buy God's gift of the Spirit, probably for his own gain.)*
- What choice did Peter make that changed the story? *(He corrected Simon. He spoke the truth about what Simon was doing.)*

SHOCKING AND SCANDALOUS STORIES FROM THE BIBLE

- **Why do you think this story is in the Bible?** *(This is an opportunity to remind students of today's Bible verse, "All these are the work of one and the same Spirit, and he gives them to each one, just as he determines" [1 Corinthians 12:11].)*

God's gifts come to us through a relationship with Jesus. We all receive the Holy Spirit. We're gifted with talents and abilities too. Money can't buy these one-of-a-kind, individually given, God-given talents. ✘

Take 3: Critics' Corner (15 to 20 minutes)

Setup: Reinforce the points you want your students to take away from today's lesson.

Props: Group journal with entries from Take 1; **Outtakes** (p. 176); red marker, small trinket

QUIET ON THE SET

Return to the group journal to review the "Money, Money, Money" questions and response entries.

ACTION

Consider the POV

Ask the group:

- Simon wanted to buy the power of the Spirit, probably so he could turn around and demand money for it. How does one evil desire often lead to another? When have you seen this idea in action?

Draw students' attention to the **POV** on the **Outtakes** handout: *Money can't buy the powerful gifts God gives us.*

Together, review the hot seat entries in the group journal and evaluate each one to see how well it reflects today's POV. Separate fact from fiction: Use a red marker to circle those entries that pass the POV test.

Ask the group:

- Imagine that God's left you in charge for the day. What prayer would you answer for another that doesn't involve money?

Jot down students' ideas about God's "priceless" gifts we live with each day. (The Holy Spirit, family, friends, love, good health, and so on.)

Understand God's Truth

Peter said what needed to be said. A pretty bold move! No one likes to be corrected. Peter was right: We can't throw money at God to get what we want. He has no use for it. God's gifts are priceless.

Ask the group:

- **What have we learned from today's story?** *(The gifts of God can't be bought.)*
- **How can we apply this to our lives?** *(We need to be content with the talents and spiritual gifts God has given us—and use them to honor him.)*

Our glorious God is eternal, endless, unchanging, all-knowing, and all-present. He is Spirit, invisible and sovereign, meaning he rules over everything. There's not enough cash in the whole world to buy that!

Teamwork

All for one and one for all. Together this week we can make a positive difference in the world we live in. Let's support and encourage each other as we live by the power of God's Holy Spirit within us.

PLAY BACK

Wrap up the meeting with a team-building guessing game that's based on today's Bible story. Then close in prayer.

Hidden Treasure

Needed: a small trinket
Goal: Try and keep the treasure from "Simon."

How to Play:

Form a group circle (God's people) and have everyone sit with their hands behind their backs. Pick someone to be "It" (Simon the Sorcerer) and have him or her stand in the middle of the circle with eyes closed. Place a small trinket (God's gifts) in a seated player's palm. When "Simon" opens his or her eyes, play begins. Players will try and pass the trinket behind backs from one hand to another, reversing direction, and pretending to pass while "Simon" tries to guess who has it. It's important for the circle players to be as still as possible and to keep a straight face so as not to give away the location of the "treasure." If the center player guesses correctly, "Simon" and the player with the trinket switch places and play continues.

Close with Prayer

Ask your group to look again at **Outtakes** and repeat today's **Key Verse**: "All these are the work of one and the same Spirit, and he gives them to each one, just as he determines" (1 Corinthians 12:11). Then point out this week's *Verse-atility: God's Spirit gives me gifts all my own.* Encourage your students to keep God's truth front and center in their lives this week. If time permits, jot the verse in the group journal and have everyone initial it.

> **Verse-atility:** *God's Spirit gives me gifts all my own.*

Listen for prayer requests, and then pray for your students. Also pray that your students would be in tune with God's Spirit as he leads them and empowers them throughout the week. ✘

> If you want, try a "Twenty-One-Hum Salute" to close your prayer time. Pick a favorite worship tune and hum it together.

Outtakes

CAST
Philip: a follower of Jesus telling people in Samaria the good news
Peter and John: followers of Jesus who come from Jerusalem to see what's happening
Simon: a man famous in Samaria for his magic

MOVIE TRAILER
- Philip comes to Samaria to tell the good news of God's kingdom.
- Many people decide to believe in Jesus and are baptized, including Simon.
- When Peter and John come, they lay hands on believers and the Holy Spirit comes to them.
- Simon tries to *buy* the power of the Spirit.
- Peter tells Simon he's got it all wrong and has to change his ways.

Verse-atility: God's Spirit gives me gifts all my own.

POV: Money can't buy the powerful gifts God gives us.
Key Verse: All these are the work of one and the same Spirit, and he gives them to each one, just as he determines (1 Corinthians 12:11).

UNDER THE INFLUENCE
Acts 8:9-24 *(The Message)*
*(We've added a few of our own comments **in bold** below.)*

Previous to Philip's arrival, a certain Simon had practiced magic in the city, posing as a famous man and dazzling all the Samaritans with his wizardry. He had them all, from little children to old men, eating out of his hand. They all thought he had supernatural powers, and called him "the Great Wizard." **[Sounds like a video game.]** He had been around a long time and everyone was more or less in awe of him.

But when Philip came to town announcing the news of God's kingdom and proclaiming the name of Jesus Christ, they forgot Simon and were baptized, becoming believers right and left! Even Simon himself believed and was baptized. From that moment he was like Philip's shadow **[Stick with the popular guy.]**, so fascinated with all the God-signs and miracles that he wouldn't leave Philip's side.

When the apostles in Jerusalem received the report that Samaria had accepted God's Message, they sent Peter and John down to pray for them to receive the Holy Spirit. Up to this point they had only been baptized in the name of the Master Jesus; the Holy Spirit hadn't yet fallen on them. Then the apostles laid their hands on them and they did receive the Holy Spirit.

When Simon saw that the apostles by merely laying on hands conferred the Spirit, he pulled out his money, excited, and said, "Sell me your secret! Show me how you did that! How much do you want? Name your price!"

Peter said, "To hell with your money! **[Peter's anger is red hot!]** And you along with it. Why, that's unthinkable—trying to buy God's gift! You'll never be part of what God is doing by striking bargains and offering bribes. Change your ways—and now! Ask the Master to forgive you for trying to use God to make money. I can see this is an old habit with you; you reek with money-lust."

"Oh!" said Simon, "pray for me! Pray to the Master that nothing like that will ever happen to me!"

Permission is granted by Standard Publishing to reproduce this **Outtakes** handout for ministry purposes only (not for resale).

Money, Money, Money

A well-off (rich!) seventh grader transfers to your school. She doesn't have any friends just yet. She invites you to go shopping—and says she'll pay for what you want to buy. You know the real reason: She wants you to be her friend. But is she trying to buy your friendship? What will you do? Why?

You owe your sister $12. She wants the money to go to the movies. Your mom pays you $15 for cleaning out the garage. Your best friend texts and invites you (*yes!*) to the movies! You can pay your sister back or use your $15 to go to the movies. What will you do? Why?

Your grandfather owns 15,000 shares in Big Bucks Gold Mine. As his heir, you stand to inherit $1 million. Should you be able to buy anything you want with the money? Why or why not?

On the corner you pass an ATM that's spewing out money. Ten-dollar bills are scattered on the sidewalk at your feet. It's just you and the cold hard cash! What will you do? Why?

You're doing laundry and find $40 in the pocket of your sister's jeans. Will you tell her? Why or why not?

Your friend sees your brother's top-of-the-line tennis racket in your garage and offers you $50 for it. It's just gathering a lot of dust, and he never seemed to use it much. Your brother is away at college. What will you do? Why?

Your aunt gives you $100 for your birthday. It's enough to get that phone or give you enough for that guitar that you want, but your mom wants you to put it in the bank. What will you do? Why?

What would it take for you to feel like you had enough money? How *much* is enough? Why?

You go to the movies and pay with a ten-dollar bill. You get all the way to your seat when you realize the clerk gave you change for a twenty. What would you do? Why?

Your friend wants you to join him in his lawn mowing business in your neighborhood. He's already got a lot of customers, and you'll make great money. But it will mean working five to six hours each Saturday. That will put a serious crunch on your weekend plans: relaxing at home, sports practice, and family time. Would you take the job? Why or why not?

Permission is granted by Standard Publishing to reproduce "Money, Money, Money" for ministry purposes only (not for resale).